Austin, Texas—Then and Now

BY

Jeffrey Kerr

Austin, Texas—Then and Now

Copyright © 2004 by Jeffrey Kerr

All rights reserved.

No part of this book may be reproduced or utilized commercially in any form or by
any means, electronic or mechanical, including photocopying, recording or by
any information storage and retrieval system, without permission in writing
from the Publisher. Inquiries should be addressed to:

Promised Land books
6805 Edgefield Drive
Austin, TX 78731

Library of Congress Cataloging-in-Publication Data

Kerr, Jeffrey
Austin, Texas—Then and Now

p.   cm.   illus.

1. Austin (Tex.)—History. 2. Austin (Tex.)—Description. 3. Texas—History.
4. Travis County (Tex.)—History. 5. Cities and towns—Growth. 6. City Planning—Texas—Austin.

I Title.   II. Authors.   III. History.   IV. Monograph.

Library of Congress Control Number 2004097092

ISBN 0-9761152-0-4 Soft cover
ISBN 0-9761152-1-2 Hard cover

F394 A988 K68   976.411 Au76ke   2004097092

Printed in the United States of America
at Morgan Printing in Austin, Texas

For my Family

TABLE OF CONTENTS

VII. Around the 40 Acres 216
"A university of the first class"

FOREWORD

Even a brief history about how Austin developed explains a great deal about why certain approaches to urban design and planning were taken and sheds light on how our attitude toward historic preservation has evolved. It is important to remember that until quite recently Austin was really a small college town and state capital. Stretching north from the Colorado River to the State Capitol grounds and sandwiched between Waller and Shoal Creeks, the well-planned original little city was a concentrated urban environment that maintained itself as such well into the early 20th century. It had its vital business district, its industrial zones, its public buildings, its public squares, its grand residential boulevards, and its working class neighborhoods. Not exceptionally wealthy or stylish or particularly progressive during its early years, Austin was a solid, normal, American hometown, not unlike state capitals and college towns all over the country. And, as in most of America, design ideas and other trends took a little longer to get here—the railroads not until 1871 and the first formal city planning not until 1928.

By the start of World War II, Austin's population was about 50,000. Its northern limits had reached all the way to 45th Street, and the southern limits had crossed the Colorado River. Within this area is what would be conventionally thought of as the "historic architecture" zone of the city, with much of it cohesive and intact until the great building boom of the late 1970s and 1980s. As the city rightfully began to gain notice for its intellectual and entrepreneurial resources, its laid-back, liberal lifestyle, and its accessible natural beauty, the combination was too temping to resist, and people, businesses, and money began to arrive as if in a great, planned migration. The city grew exponentially, especially to the far north and west and, for perhaps the first time in history,

Austinites could live complete lives that never brought them into contact with the historic core of the city. As schools, government offices, and satellite public services fanned out toward the edges of the county, "old Austin" just ceased to be a part of the orbit of many folks. Fortunately, the historic preservation movement in Austin hit its stride about this same time, and it was the period of greatest influence for the visionary bankers, businesses, arts organizations, and historical groups who moved deftly to save entire neighborhoods—from the Bremond Block to Sixth Street to portions of Congress Avenue and the University of Texas campus—and to rescue pivotal buildings and sites from destruction, preserving the key landmarks and areas that defined the city's very character. Of course, there have been many losses, and some of them are documented in this extraordinarily well-done book. New York Times architecture critic Ada Louise Huxtable predicted in the 1970s that historic preservation would have the greatest impact upon American architecture and our cities in the late 20th century. Austin is surely proof of that, beginning with the entertainment and hospitality industries and continuing on its course to revitalize the inner city for another generation of retail, commercial, and residential life.

True historic preservationists share essentially the same goals as true environmentalists: quality of life for now and for the future. Just as environmentalists want to preserve open land to offset too-rapid encroachment of development, historic preservationists seek to create a balance between the human scale of the past and the increasingly "supersized" scale of the world that is offered to us daily in the name of progress or a strong economy. To preservationists, an abandoned, decaying building or site speaks of our social and aesthetic decay much the way a toxic waste dump, a polluted aquifer, or an eroding landscape speaks of our failure to protect our own habitat and thus our very future. There is much more relevance to historic preservation than most citizens realize. I am therefore offering a broader definition of historic preservationists as "built environmentalists" with the primary focus on those human-made buildings, sites, structures, and spaces which define our specific community character and culture. Sometimes these resources appear in the form of individual landmarks, usually architectural gems of grand scale and opulence. Other times there is a larger, more sweeping importance like a neighborhood, a farm, a park, or a bridge. Not often enough it is the row of small houses in a working class neighborhood or the mom-and-pop grocery store on the corner that finds a place on our "most cherished" list. In the decades of the 1920s and 30s, two of America's most historic cities, Charleston, SC, and New Orleans, LA, founded their preservation movements from the very beginning focused on the ensembles of buildings, structures, and sites, rather than on individual landmarks. In New Orleans, this "tout ensemble" concept preserved one our country's most unique cultural and urban environments in the Vieux Carre. In fact, when you think of the most historic cities in America, don't you think of them in terms of their wholeness rather than their individual buildings? Even those benefactors obsessed with individual landmarks recognized the need to preserve context, and in the 1930s Colonial Williamsburg was born to teach us about living, design, and continuity in an earlier time. We as a nation got the basic principles of preservation but not all the core concepts, however, and began treating symptoms but not the causes of our cities' decaying fabric. After World War II, planning for national historic preservation movement set out, not to restore and preserve a way of life, but to isolate, preserve and/or reconstruct idealized villages, military sites, battlefields, and the mansions of rich, white men. But there was a different paradigm at work across the Atlantic. Architects, planners, civic and spiritual leaders first sought to restore the iconography of their war-ravaged cities'

streetscapes, parks, and plazas rather than just its major landmarks. The urban context—the continuity and cohesiveness of place—was more important to the quality of their lives and to the future of their culture than any single building. To boost their spirits and provide collective energy to recreate their lives, the Europeans needed their past in order to provide a future that was truly their own.

So what does all this have to do with Austin, Texas, and this marvelous collection of historic and contemporary photographs? In a remarkable feat of research, analysis, and fieldwork, not to mention top-notch photography, Jeff Kerr has provided us with a different kind of local history. Using carefully selected images from public and private collections, Dr. Kerr has created a documentary of our city's physical self—reaching back a century and more—to tell us about and show us the buildings, streets, parks, and open spaces that Austinites built to define themselves. It is, in effect, a visual résumé of our dreams, aspirations, successes, and defeats, our flush times, and our hard times. Some people paging through this collection will feel pangs of nostalgia for the places of childhood memories; others will revel in the richness and beauty of the architecture and streetscapes. There will also be sighs of anguish or disbelief from the comparison of Austin then and Austin now—"How could we have let this happen?" or "Thank goodness, we don't have that problem anymore."

But the cumulative experience of these images, old and new, is much more surprising and profound. We cannot view them without asking ourselves some provocative questions. Have we been good stewards of the city we've inherited? Do we design our new buildings, streets, and public places as part of an ensemble or merely a string of unrelated developments? Have we abandoned our unique character in exchange for something else? Have we truly included our past in our future? Jeff Kerr has accompanied his selections and excellent new photographs with an elegant and unobtrusive text—enough to provide appropriate and accurate context, just enough to make you want to learn more. He wants the images to teach us, to inspire us to look at our city—as it was and as it is now—and take more seriously the decisions we make that affect its appearance and to get involved in what happens next. This is not your grandparents' local history, although they will enjoy it immensely. And this is not just a picture book. Ultimately, this is a book for the "built environmentalist" in all of us. It challenges us to think about the physical world immediately around us. How we respond to our visual environment will determine how successfully we take our city into the future.

Gregory Free
October 2004

INTRODUCTION

No one in the mighty army camped on the south Texas prairie of San Jacinto expected the onslaught which destroyed them. The rising sun spread its morning warmth over a sleepy collection of 1500 well-armed men confident in the strength conveyed by superior numbers. Led by the charismatic Antonio Lopez de Santa Anna, head-of-state of the Republic of Mexico, the men slept or lolled sleepily about camp on the morning of April 21, 1836, preparing for a day of certain victory over the pirates attempting to steal their nation's northern province of Texas. These bandits had fought poorly, or not at all, in the several weeks since brazenly declaring independence from the country whose friendship they now betrayed. After their comrades suffered obliteration at the Alamo in San Antonio, and again on a plain near Goliad, the remaining Texian rebels had turned and run, barely keeping up with their commander, General Sam Houston, in what seemed like a headlong flight to Louisiana.

But now they were trapped. Fronted by an army twice the size of their own, the Texians were cut off from retreat by Buffalo Bayou to their rear. Never mind the marsh known as Peggy's Lake to the Mexicans' own rear or the San Jacinto River on the army's right flank. Santa Anna need not concern himself with the usual military considerations in the face of such an inferior opponent. In short order, perhaps after breakfast, he would unleash the fury of his forces upon his despicable foes, whose bodies he could then have stacked and burned as he had done after the Alamo conquest.

Imagine then the utter astonishment on the faces of the first Mexican soldiers to die as the bullets whistled in from the line of screaming men charging over the small rise between the two armies. Those Mexicans who didn't immediately flee soon joined their dead comrades as they were bayoneted, shot, or clubbed to death. The few feeble attempts at organized resistance rapidly disintegrated. Surviving soldiers then paid the price of their commander's folly. From dry ground Texian marksmen fired, reloaded, and fired again into the mass of panicked Mexicans struggling through Peggy's Lake. Some drowned, others begged for mercy as they were slaughtered by the revenge-driven killers before them. By the time Texian passions had cooled several hundred Mexicans lay dead in the muck. Nine Texans perished.

Thus did Sam Houston achieve glory as the man credited with winning Texas' independence from Mexico. Who then but the hero of San Jacinto as first President of the new Republic of Texas? The former general formed a government in the recently established town of Harrisburg, on the banks of Buffalo Bayou. He envisioned this settlement, later renamed Houston in his honor, as the permanent capital of the nation.

But his vice president, Mirabeau B. Lamar, had other ideas.

Lamar dreamed of a vast Texan empire, whose western extent would be limited only by the imaginations of those in power. To confine the capital of this future great nation in its southeastern corner seemed to him folly. How could the expanding frontier be governed from such distance? Better to find a central location allowing greater access to the western regions.

Such thoughts occupied the Vice President's mind as he accepted an invitation from his friend Jacob Harrell in 1838 to hunt buffalo in the vicinity of the Colorado River settlement of Waterloo. Harrell had been the first white man to risk a home so far up the river, having moved from the Hornsby settlement to the east not long before. Lamar arrived with an escort of Texas Rangers, then set up camp at the mouth of Shoal Creek, close to Harrell's stockaded cabin.

The following morning Harrell's son burst excitedly in on the men with news of nearby buffalo. Quickly astride their mounts, Lamar, Harrell and the Rangers sped off to the northeast in pursuit of the herd. Galloping first up the banks of the creek bed, the party crossed a short grassy plain, then followed a gentle slope down into a ravine leading up from the river. There, at what is now the intersection of 8th Street and Congress Avenue in the city of Austin, Vice President Lamar felled an enormous buffalo, the largest ever seen by the men in his company. Later, after gathering to the bugle call with the rest of the hunters atop a rise to the north, Lamar gazed admiringly at the surrounding scenery and exclaimed, "This should be the seat of future empire!"

Shortly after reading this story for the first time, I visited downtown Austin to stand on the spot of the unfortunate buffalo's demise. As I gazed north to the Capitol and all around me at tall buildings new and old, I was struck by the drastically different appearance the landscape offers in modern times. I tried to picture first the treeless vista Lamar would have enjoyed as he stood over his trophy and gazed toward the Colorado River to the south. Then I imagined the row of log structures which soon appeared along newly laid-out Congress Avenue. I was saddened that nothing remains as a physical link to the city's birth.

But I was wrong. It occurred to me that standing at 8th and Congress, I could visually trace exactly the same sloping terrain down to the waterfront that inspired Lamar. I could turn around and see the same hill conceptualized by urban planner and Lamar friend Edwin Waller as the perfect site for the Republic's Capitol building. I could walk east to the banks of Waller Creek or west to Shoal Creek and dip a hand into the waters of Austin's natural original boundaries.

A stroll down Congress Avenue between the Capitol and the Colorado River (now tamed by Longhorn Dam and renamed Town Lake) opened my eyes to numerous surviving links with Austin's past. Many 19th century structures survive. The Robinson-Rosner building at 504 Congress dates to 1856, just 17 years removed from Austin's founding. Historical markers informed me of saloons, opera houses, and livery stables operating long ago in buildings now housing law firms and restaurants. Just east of Congress on 6th Street, across from the Driskill Hotel, I stumbled across an iron hitching ring in the sidewalk, a vital amenity for shoppers on old Pecan Street in an equestrian age.

Excited by these discoveries, I headed to the Austin History Center to look for photographs depicting Austin as it looked in early days. A mountain of material awaited me. Over the ensuing months I passed countless hours thumbing through the stacks of pictorial files cheerfully provided by helpful staff members. "Other people should see this," I thought. At that time I had lived in Austin for twelve years and had no idea that so many of the city's historic structures remained. True, much had also been destroyed, but having grown up in another Texas city which preserved very little of its past, I was thrilled. Conversations with friends taught me that many Austinites shared my weak grasp of the significance of local historic sites and buildings encountered daily.

Roots are important to me. I returned to Texas in 1991 after five years in beautiful North Carolina because of the pull of memories and loved ones. Gazing at physical links to the past, touching stones worked by some of Austin's original citizens, staring in awe at an orange sun setting over the same purple hills that inspired the author O. Henry, hearing my footsteps in hallways once frequented by those for whom the city's streets are named, all serve to deepen my own feelings of respect and love for my home. My inspiration for writing this book is to invite others to share these charms.

My photographs are an attempt to precisely portray the modern view of each historic scene presented. This was not always possible. Trees, obstructing buildings, reluctant property owners, altered topography, and modern traffic provided impediments. In accompanying text I have provided orientation to the scene as well as historical context of notable structures and persons. The reader will note striking similarities between many of the paired photographs.

Absence of surviving landmarks in other comparisons are testimony to the importance of preservation.

Austin, Texas: Then and Now is not intended as a history book. Nor is it a collection of artistic photographs. Where aesthetics conflicted with accuracy in re-depicting the visual past, I chose the latter. Instead, I present a scrapbook of Austin scenery, which may serve to strengthen our ties to those who preceded us, and our sense of responsibility to those whom *we* precede.

Jeffrey Kerr
September 2004

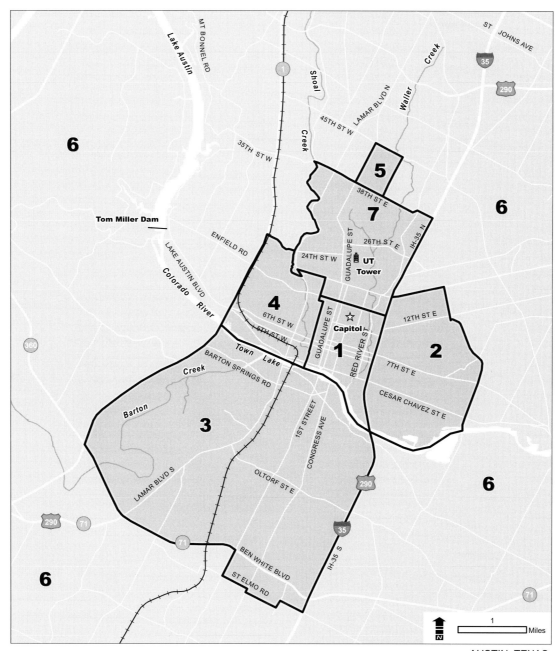

AUSTIN, TEXAS

I. BETWEEN THE CREEKS

Within Edwin Waller's Original Boundaries

"This should be the seat of future empire!"

— Mirabeau B. Lamar, first Vice President, Republic of Texas,
on a buffalo hunt near the mouth of Shoal Creek on the Colorado River

*". . . a prairie containing perhaps two thousand acres, composed of a chocolate colored sandy loam,
intersected by two beautiful streams of permanent and pure water. . .
This section of country is generally well watered, fertile in a high degree,
and has every appearance of health and salubrity of climate."*

— Report of the Capital site selection commission 1839

Stand today under the ancient live oaks in Austin's Republic Square and imagine the frenzied scene on that spot over a century and a half ago. Shaded from the hot August sun by these same trees, Judge Edwin Waller faced an excited crowd of "good, staunch, and hardy citizens" and presided over the first public sale of lots in the intended Texas capital city. Since June 1839 Waller had been urging on a crew of 200 workmen responsible for the row of log structures visible to the east. These pitifully small buildings lined a ravine optimistically labeled "Congress Avenue" in Waller's city plan. Commanding the ravine's western embankment was the republic's new capitol, an unimpressive one-story wooden building 60 by 115 feet. Across the ravine stood the presidential "mansion," actually a two-story frame house soon to be occupied by new president Mirabeau Lamar. Other recently constructed houses in the area, occupying as yet unacquired land, emphasized the importance of the auction's outcome to many in the crowd.

Assigned the task by President Lamar, Judge Waller had laid out a grid of streets 14 blocks square which fronted the Colorado River between Shoal and Waller creeks. Capitol Square claimed the four blocks commanding the view south down Congress Avenue toward the river, the same view admired by Lamar on his buffalo hunt the previous year. Waller named the western and eastern boundaries of his grid West and East avenues. Except for Congress Avenue he used the names of major Texas rivers for north-south streets in between. Over Waller's objections most of the streets running parallel to the river were named after Texas trees. Exceptions included North Street (now 15th), Water Street (now Cesar Chavez) and College Avenue (now 12th). Waller preferred merely using numbers as street names, a recommendation the city finally adopted in 1887, six years after Waller's death.

By day's end August 1, 1839, Judge Waller had accepted winning bids on 306 lots, selling for a total of $182,588. One hundred twenty dollars was good enough for the least expensive lot; the most expensive demanded more than 23 times that amount. Not a bad profit for the Republic, which had paid a little over $20,000 for the 7,735 acres selected by the capital commission, of which the area in Waller's city plan was only a small part.

AUSTIN, TEXAS

From the seed of Edwin Waller's 14-block square thus grew the urban metropolis that is today's Austin. Still the heart of the city, and arguably of the state, downtown remains home to the city hospital, City Hall, police headquarters, the county courthouse and jail, several churches, businesses, museums, banks, an elementary school, a community college, and the main city library. Although most single-family dwellings in the area disappeared long ago, a recent surge of interest in downtown living has stimulated construction of multiple residential towers. The beautiful 19th-century Capitol Building (the city's fourth) still sparkles as the centerpiece of downtown Austin, indeed of the entire city.

The historic photographs in this section date back to the 1860s, and thus almost back to that day when Judge Waller stood sweating under a hot August sun. How different the Austin of today! And yet, amid the gleaming glass and steel survive numerous landmarks Edwin Waller would have recognized. Enjoy finding them in the pages that follow.

Courtesy of Austin History Center, Austin Public Library PICA 02443

1. Congress Avenue Bridge, looking north toward the Capitol
c.1890

Edwin Waller laid out the major thoroughfare of the Republic's new capital city to follow a ravine leading up from the Colorado River to the plateau from which Mirabeau Lamar had dreamed of future empire. One suspects Lamar would have been pleased by this sweeping view toward the majestic new Capitol Building atop the rise a half-century later. Nineteenth-century pedestrians mingle with horse-drawn wagons and carriages along a broad Congress Avenue lined with busy shops, professional offices, and hotels. The Capitol's dome towers above the downtown landscape without competition from the skyscrapers of the future. Boasting of "a convenient location for all" the Colorado House at right rented rooms for a dollar a day in 1889. Weekly and monthly rates were also available.

Congress Avenue Bridge, looking north toward the Capitol
2004

Modern bridge pedestrians still enjoy the unobstructed view of the Capitol, but little else seems unchanged in this photograph. The Scarbrough Building at center left (with Texas flag) was the first modern skyscraper to challenge the Capitol dome's skyline dominance. Looming from behind is One America Center, first of a new breed of downtown giants built during a 1980s building boom which destroyed many Austin landmarks. Newest of these titanic structures is the city's tallest building, the Frost Bank Tower at right. Partially obstructing a view of the tower is the Radisson Hotel, erected on the site of the old Colorado House. Pedestrians now must keep to the sidewalks in deference to traffic more dangerous than that in former times.

23

Courtesy of Austin History Center, Austin Public Library C00308

2. Cypress Street, looking west at Congress Avenue
c.1880

When the International and Great Northern Railroad (I&GN) reached Austin from Palestine in 1876, the depot on the southwest corner at 3rd Street and Congress Avenue quickly became one of the busiest spots in town. Arriving passengers relied on private transfer wagons or mule-drawn streetcars for transportation to a hotel. Those awaiting departing trains could relax in the depot restaurant or in one of the many nearby saloons (center right). Austin's western hills are clearly visible beyond the low-lying skyline. Such a view west from town at sunset supposedly inspired O. Henry to dub Austin "the City of the Violet Crown" in his 1894 short story *Tictocq, the Great French Detective, in Austin.*

3rd Street, looking west at Congress Avenue
2004

City residents must have beamed with pride in 1888 upon reading an *Austin Daily Statesman* article boasting, "Austin is to have the most complete and beautiful depot in the state. . . the building will be located on the site of the shanty that for years has been doing duty as a depot. . . ." More than six decades later dwindling ridership doomed not only the passenger trains, but also the landmark structure built in their service. Since the 1950s only a drab parking lot has marked the spot of earlier railway glory. Although Congress Avenue itself retains its bustling nature, its intersection at 3rd Street today offers nothing to remind current residents of its one-time importance to Austin.

Courtesy of Austin History Center, Austin Public Library PICA 18667

Courtesy of Austin History Center, Austin Public Library

**3a. Congress Avenue at Cypress Street, northeast corner
1886**

**3b. Congress Avenue at 3rd Street, northeast corner
c.1900**

Mrs. Eliza Knight picked an ideal location for her 19th-century Union Depot boarding house. Located on the northeast corner of 3rd Street and Congress Avenue, the house lay alongside tracks for the Houston and Texas Central Railroad, and thus was among the first sights to greet arriving city visitors. In this photograph Mrs. Knight stands at far left next to daughter Hattie (seated), while 10-year-old son George surveys Congress Avenue from a second-story window of his mother's hotel. Modern viewers may be startled by the residential appearance of the downtown property, as conveyed by the picket fence and multiple tall trees. Eliza Knight came to Texas from Rochester, New York in 1875 with her father, Leonard Dill. Dill and Eliza's brother William operated a carriage harness business in Austin. After Eliza's death in 1888, her two children were sent back to Rochester, where George lived the rest of his life. Reminiscing in 1945, George recalled that the popular boarding house "always did a good business."

After the euphoria accompanying the arrival of rail service to Austin in 1871 had worn off local residents began calling for better facilities. In 1878 the *Austin Statesman* complained, "It is thought that the Central intends putting up a fine depot after awhile—in the course of ten or fifteen years." Two decades later the city still waited, but this time the *Statesman* had better news to report: "Austin's new Union depot will be a magnificent ornament to the city when completed." But the rival newspaper *Austin Daily Tribune* commented upon a phenomenon familiar to 21st-century Austinites, "The delay in beginning work is partly due to the little legal formalities that have to be complied with. Let the good work go on." In 1898, after Austin had waited for 33 years, the new H&TC depot opened on the site of Eliza Knight's old Union Depot House, which had been demolished earlier that year. Capital city residents returning from Houston with their $5.40 round-trip ticket could at last look forward to stepping off the train onto a modern, shaded platform.

Congress Avenue at 3rd Street, northeast corner
2004

Remarking in 1965 on the razing of what by then was known as the Southern Pacific Depot, the *Austin American-Statesman* pointed out the obvious cause of the building's destruction, "And now we ride the train as novelty, not a necessity." In fact, because the structure had already stood vacant for 13 years many Austin residents agreed with the sign placed by the demolition company as workers completed their task, "Keep the Ball of Progress Rolling." At the grand opening of its new 22-story office tower in November 1986, builder Trammell Crow

Company displayed artifacts recovered during excavation of the construction site. Attendees marveled at items ranging from two square brown bottles marked "Dr. J. Hostetter's Stomach Bitter" to a 17,000-year-old mammoth bone. At least one local newspaper columnist was favorably impressed by the new skyscraper. Describing the building as "lyrical and light on its feet," *American-Statesman* writer Michael McCuller added that the "winner" of "the Great Congress Avenue High-Rise Race . . . is plain to see."

Courtesy of Austin History Center, Austin Public Library PICA 02460

4. Congress Avenue, looking north at 3rd Street
1905

As the twentieth century dawned, residents of the capital of Texas still contended with the dust and mud inherent to dirt streets. Here a trench crew helps prepare Congress Avenue for a welcomed improvement, the laying of paving bricks. Businesses such as John Orr's grocery in the W.B. Smith Building (1884) and C.J. Martin Hay, Grain, and Seed in the Koppel Building (1888) paid for paving along their fronts. The city covered the cost of paving the intersections. Tracks along the Avenue's center first saw service in January 1875 when directors of the Austin City Railway Company boarded a mule-drawn streetcar for an inaugural ride. Rounding the curve at Congress Avenue and 11th Street the car derailed, and embarrassed directors tumbled unceremoniously into the street. In 1891 the Austin Rapid Transit Railway Company began operating the first electric cars on the Avenue. Company founder Monroe Shipe needed a system of efficient public transportation to entice people to move north to his new Hyde Park subdivision. Although power-killing floods occasionally interfered with the running of the cars, the company persisted and was able to benefit greatly from a fire later that year which destroyed the barn housing the city's mule-drawn cars. Sixteen cars and at least 30 mules were lost.

Congress Avenue, looking north at 3rd Street
2004

Today concrete covers the century-old paving bricks of Congress Avenue. Streetcar tracks served their country during World War II as scrap metal after being removed in 1940. Still looking for the ideal public transportation system, the city in recent years has twice seen light-rail referendums defeated at the polls. Envious of successful rail service in cities such as Dallas and Portland, Oregon, local proponents continue their efforts to bring a street rail system back to Austin. At left, although John Orr and C.J. Martin have left the Avenue, the ornate buildings which housed their business enterprises remain.

Courtesy of Austin History Center, Austin Public Library PICA 25586

5. Congress Avenue at 4th Street, southeast corner
post-1869

Thirsty Austinites welcomed Dawson and King's opening of the first "bar room" in their city on this site in 1840. In 1869 the Austin Building Association erected the building pictured here in an attempt to entice the United States Army to base its 5th Military District in Austin. Civic pride received a blow when the army opted instead for San Antonio, in part because Austin still awaited rail service. Dr. M. A. Taylor then leased the vacant building from local government and opened the Raymond House hotel in January 1871. The *Austin Statesman* reported an on-site brawl later that year between members of the Texas Legislature who had "congregated to 'relax'. . . . Order was finally restored, but without no other personage than the governor himself whose interference was beseeched by the management." Owners undertook an extensive remodeling in 1874. The *Daily Democratic Statesman* boasted that "the Raymond House, the pride of Austin" [is adding] "door bells, which will enable a guest in any room in the house to summon a waiter from the office by simply pulling a little knob." A room rate reduction from $3.50 to $3.00 per day was cited as further evidence that "Mr. Adam has an eye to the comfort of his guests."

Congress Avenue at 4th Street, southeast corner
2004

The Raymond House closed in 1888. W.T. Wroe then moved his saddle and harness business into the building. The Austin City Directory described Wroe as "a practical man in every way" whose "enterprise is doing much to spread abroad the reputation of Austin as a producing center as well as a delightful place of residence." By 1912 Hicks Tire Company occupied the site. Later, a car dealership gave way to Karotkin Furniture Company, which financed the structure's last major renovation in 1933-1934. Karotkin's was replaced by Barker Office Furniture in 1974. In 1988 the Mexic-Arte Museum moved in, attracted in part by the Congress Avenue location. The museum's current desire for a larger facility threatens this Austin landmark with demolition. Protective historic designation was denied by City Council in deference to the museum.

6a. Congress Avenue, looking north at 5th Street
1913

Cattleman George Littlefield followed Scarbrough with his own skyscraper in 1911, of which the *Austin Statesman* exclaimed "nothing in Texas can begin to compare with it." The same report extolled the advantages of the new "business home" over a more mundane "office building" in that, in the former, "every convenience is at hand . . . business, when transacted at a business home, is a joy and not a drudge." Littlefield's own American National Bank occupied much of the ground floor. The eighth floor roof was originally a popular garden, intended as "the mecca of citizens and visitors during summer months" with its "moving picture exhibitions or theatrical performances." Littlefield eliminated the garden when he added another story in 1915, and Austinites had to look elsewhere for their summer entertainment.

6b. Congress Avenue, looking north at 5th Street
1960s

Austin's two new marvels, the Scarbrough Building (left) and the Littlefield Building (right) frame this view of Congress Avenue. Although the Scarbrough Building opened first in 1910, one reporter gushed that it was the 1911 opening of the Littlefield Building which marked "the closing of the provincial or town era of the city of Austin and the beginning of the metropolitan or city era of this place." Both structures employed the new technique of steel frame construction, the technological breakthrough enabling the erection of such tall edifices.

Emerson Scarbrough opened his dry goods store Scarbrough and Hicks on the Avenue in 1892. R.H. Hicks, Scarbrough's partner since 1883, remained in Rockdale to run the duo's original enterprise. The *Austin Statesman* praised Scarbrough as "a shining example of what may be accomplished through the proper application of energy and industry." His new "entirely modern" skyscraper boasted marble stairways, terrazzo floors, three elevator cars (one for exclusive use between the store's two floors), "hot and cold water in every room," and a cooling system involving air circulated over refrigerating pipes.

Surprisingly, by the 1960s Austin's two original skyscrapers were still among the tallest on Congress Avenue. Peeking over the Scarbrough Building at far left though is the Norwood Tower, which eclipsed all other Austin office buildings in height at its opening in 1929. Norwood Tower boasted air-conditioning (a first for Austin) and a "Motoramp" garage, in which automobiles rode an elevator to reach the appropriate parking level. Behind the Littlefield Building at right is the Stephen F. Austin Hotel, which hosted its first guests in 1924.

Congress Avenue, looking north at 5th Street
2004

In 1984 construction of the 33-story One American Center (at left behind the Scarbrough Building) heralded a new era of tall buildings on Congress Avenue. A debate regarding whether to allow the Capitol to be blocked from view by such facilities resulted in the local concept of protected "view corridors." As can be seen, however, this did not prevent development of other massive structures. The view north on Congress Avenue below the Capitol provides one of the few remaining unobstructed views of the building which once dominated Austin's landscape. Emerson Scarbrough's business still peddles stylish clothing to capital city residents, but since 1994 from a new location on North Lamar Boulevard. Nevertheless, Scarbrough's namesake building, as well as the contemporary Littlefield Building across the street, continue as thriving "business homes" on Congress Avenue.

Courtesy of Center for American History, UT-Austin CN Number 02075

Looking-up- Congress- Avenue- 1876
State- Capitol- at- head- of- Avenue

7a. Congress Avenue, looking north at Pecan Street
1876

Congress Avenue was laid out in 1839 as the main commercial artery of the city, to be commanded from atop a natural ridge by the future state Capitol. That Capitol building, which was completed in 1853, replaced the original log statehouse on the northeast corner of 8th Street and Colorado Street. Never a beloved landmark, the awkward-looking building was described by one visitor as "a corn-crib with the half of a large watermelon on top of it." An 1881 fire destroyed the Greek Revival edifice. The Sampson & Henricks building on the west side of Congress Avenue was built in 1859, making it one of the first stone structures on the city's main thoroughfare.

Courtesy of Austin History Center, Austin Public Library C00639

7b. Congress Avenue, looking north at 6th Street
c. 1910

This photograph was taken from the Scarbrough Building shortly after it opened in 1909. Note the numerous churches in this downtown view, including Southern Presbyterian Church (1), St. Mary's Catholic Church (2), and M.E. South Church (3). The General Land Office (4) is seen on the southeast corner of the Capitol grounds. In the distance, to the left of the Capitol Building, is the Old Main Building of the University of Texas (5).

Congress Avenue, looking north at 6th Street
2004

Construction of the Scarbrough and Littlefield buildings nine decades earlier began the era of the skyscraper's dominance of Austin's downtown landscape. Hotels, banks, and office towers have replaced many, but not all, of the more modest structures of a bygone era. Churchgoers still worship at St. Mary's Cathedral and Southern Presbyterian Church (renamed Central Presbyterian Church). The Sampson & Henricks Building remains but is obscured by One America Center, which now takes up almost all of the west side of Congress Avenue between 5th Street and 6th Street. The Bremond Building, built by banker Eugene Bremond in 1886, is seen behind the State Theater sign. Streetcar tracks were removed after gasoline-powered buses took over public transportation in 1940.

Courtesy of Austin History Center, Austin Public Library C02096

8. Congress Avenue, looking north at 7th Street
1918

Victorious doughboys parade down Congress Avenue between two of Austin's most storied theaters. The Majestic Theater (tallest building at right) originated with wealthy lumberman Ernest Nalle in 1915. Stars such as Harry Houdini, Lillian Gish, the Barrymores, John Philip Sousa, and George M. Cohan appeared at the Majestic, which also featured motion pictures. Major George Littlefield bought the Casino Theater across the Avenue for $40,000 in 1920. Littlefield subsequently spent an additional $200,000 constructing a much larger entertainment palace, which he named the Queen Theater. The first theater in Austin built exclusively for screening motion pictures, the Queen accommodated 1200 spectators.

Congress Avenue, looking north at 7th Street
2004

The Majestic's new owner Carl Hoblitzelle renamed his theater Paramount in 1930. After a major restoration in 1980, the landmark building still breathes life into the Austin theater scene. George Littlefield's Queen was not so fortunate. During its 35-year run the theater screened such milestone films as *The Jazz Singer* and a re-released *Birth of a Nation.* After the credits rolled November 6, 1955, for *The Gun That Won the West,* the first theater in Austin built exclusively for motion pictures donated its projectors, sound amplifiers, and movie screen to the Texas School for the Deaf and closed its doors for good.

Courtesy of Austin History Center, Austin Public Library PICH 00322

9. Congress Avenue at Bois d'Arc Street, southwest corner
post-1859

When George Washington Sampson teamed up with his brother-in-law Abram Henricks in about 1850 to buy and sell local real estate, one of the first moves made by the new firm was to acquire the Orleans House on the southwest corner of Congress Avenue and Bois d'Arc Street. After this building was demolished in April 1859, Sampson and Henricks enlisted builder Abner Cook to construct the dignified edifice shown here. The following year the two friends moved the dry goods business they had begun in 1857 into the building. An article in the *State Gazette* forecast that Sampson and Henricks would be "one of the finest and largest stores in the State . . . ." At left is silversmith Adolph Bahn's shop, which promised customers in an 1872 advertisement that "watches and jewelry [would be] repaired at the shortest notice and at moderate prices."

Congress Avenue at 7th Street, southwest corner
2004

Abram Henricks died in 1865. By the late 1870s George Sampson was spending most of his time managing his extensive real estate holdings, leaving operation of the dry goods business primarily up to his new partner Ben Henricks. From 1881 until his death in 1888 Sampson leased most of his Congress Avenue building to Matthew Kreisle, who sold furniture, dry goods, carpeting, and musical instruments. Thereafter Sampson's widow leased the building to a number of businesses over the years, a practice which resulted in significant changes in its appearance. In 1982 owner George Nalle, grandson of George Sampson, leased the landmark structure to Rust Properties. This gave control of the entire west side of Congress Avenue between 6th Street and 7th Street to the development company, since it had already purchased the rest of the block. The Heritage Society of Austin hosted a gala celebrating the reopening of the restored Sampson-Henricks Building in November 1983. Rust Properties completed the high-rise office tower next door the following year. The Sampson-Henricks Building today houses a restaurant and several professional offices.

Courtesy of Austin History Center, Austin Public Library C00305

10. Congress Avenue, west side between 7th Street and 8th Street
c. 1910

Gushing once again about an upcoming "magnificent edifice" which would "be an ornament to our growing city," the *Austin Daily Statesman* in 1876 informed its readers of Walter Tips' plan for a "mammoth store building" on Congress Avenue. Prussian-born Tips arrived in Austin with his brother Edward in 1857 and founded a hardware business shortly thereafter. His $30,000 building housing his "immense" operation is the tallest structure in this photograph. To the immediate right is Clement Reed Johns' 1870 Gothic Revival building (Jesse French Piano Company). Johns operated a real estate and collection agency. At far right is the Townsend-Thompson Building. Nathaniel Thompson built a wood-frame grocery, drug, and hardware store on the site in 1841. Thaddeus Austin Thompson, envoy to Columbia in the Wilson administration, completed the Italianate Victorian structure in the photograph in 1875.

Congress Avenue, west side between 7th Street and 8th Street
2004

All three historic buildings suffered drastic alterations to their facades, only to be restored by subsequent owners. Congress Avenue Booksellers moved into a newly renovated Townsend-Thompson Building in 1983. Competition from large chain stores forced the independent bookstore out of business in 2000. Later occupant Pango Tea Shop closed in January 2004 after its owner was arrested for placing video surveillance equipment in the woman's bathroom. Insurance man John Barclay spent over $100,000 in 1981 to restore the Johns-Hamilton Building's former Gothic appearance. Franklin Savings acquired the Tips Building in 1978 from the Austin Heritage Society, which had purchased it the year before. Three years later, a parade led by Walter Tips' own carriage entertained a crowd of hundreds gathered to celebrate the building's reopening. Mayor Carole Keeton McClellan proudly announced, "we have a healthy inner city, and it will get healthier while we manage to retain the rich heritage of our past." The younger, but equally historic 1923 Norwood Tower matches the Gothic tenor of the Johns-Hamilton Building from behind. At far left the Sampson-Henricks Building (1859) survived the demolition of almost an entire city block, carried out to accommodate One America Center.

Courtesy of Austin History Center, Austin Public Library PICA 26682

11. Congress Avenue, east side between Hickory Street and Ash Street
1860s

In 1841 the General Sam Houston stagecoach braved deep-rutted roads, hostile Indians, and desperate outlaws on its inaugural trip between Austin and Brenham. Drawn by six mules in good weather and eight in bad (although only four appear in the photograph), the stagecoach in early days never traveled without armed guards to protect the mail and passengers.

Until the railroad arrived in 1871, Austin residents rode either their own horses or a coach such as this when journeying between cities. Behind the Sam Houston is Baker and Raymond Drug and Bookstore, sellers of "drugs, paints, oils, books & stationery, wall paper, fancy goods, & notions." Next door A.S. Roberts offered free delivery of "new and fresh groceries."

Congress Avenue, east side between 8th Street and 9th Street
2004

After 36 years of tolerating its presence, city government finally ordered the removal of an old stagecoach from an alley behind Patterson's Livery Stable in 1909. When those attempting to fulfill the mandate discovered that the General Sam Houston was so dilapidated it could not be moved, they had no choice but to tear it apart and throw its remains onto a scrap heap. Onlookers marveled at the numerous bullet holes in the rotting wood.

The *Austin Statesman* lamented that "another page in Texas history that can not be rewritten has been destroyed forever." After the stagecoach made its final trip between San Antonio and Austin in 1873, "it was abandoned and had to get out of the way, for the railroad took its place, and now it had to be taken out of the alley because it was deemed unsightly and in the way." Note that one-half of the former drug store and grocery building remains.

Courtesy of Austin History Center, Austin Public Library PICA 00284

12. Congress Avenue between 9th Street and 10th Street, looking southwest
1910

More than half a century after organization of the first fire protection company in Austin the business of fighting the city's fires remained largely in the hands of volunteers. In 1881 *Texas Siftings* had commented "The most prominent bankers, merchants, and professional men in Austin are firemen." Twenty-nine years later, as Austinites gathered to watch this Fireman's Parade on Congress Avenue, little had changed. Fire companies sprang into existence when enough men in a neighborhood united in the cause of protecting their homes and businesses. As the age of motorized transport dawned, all Austin fire-fighting

vehicles remained horse-drawn. Several other features in the landscape, however, indicate a city keeping up with the times. Electric lights line the Avenue, while electric streetcars continuously carry passengers along Austin's main thoroughfare. At far left rises the skeleton of the Scarbrough Building (1), first skyscraper in town. Moving north the more traditional Sampson-Henricks Building (2) stands tallest among its immediate neighbors but is topped by the Tips Building with its rounded facade (3). At far right a row of Italianate buildings designed by Jacob Larmour houses a variety of businesses.

Congress Avenue between 9th Street and 10th Street, looking southwest
2004

Nearly a century later and not a horse in sight! Austin obtained its first motorized fire-fighting vehicle in 1912 from Webb Motor Fire Apparatus Company for $4,200. In a May 1916 city election, voters approved the creation of a full-time force. Shortly thereafter 27 professional firefighters began operations under Chief Clarence Woodward. Today's department protects the city with over 1,000 employees and more than 200 vehicles.

The city implemented what many residents viewed as modernization by replacing streetcars with buses in 1940. Congress Avenue streetlights now shine from sidewalks rather than the street's center. The Scarbrough Building, Sampson-Henricks Building, and Tips Building yield in height but not beauty to several newer towers. Only Liberty Bank interrupts the graceful flow of Jacob Larmour's block at right.

Courtesy of Austin History Center, Austin Public Library PICH 01530

13. Congress Avenue at 10th Street, northwest corner
c. 1880

"A large eagle, with outstretched wings, and carved out of solid stone by that excellent mechanic, Mr. John Didelot, was yesterday elevated to the top of Mr. Lundberg's bakery building, at the head of the Avenue." Surely this report in the March 26, 1876, *Austin Statesman* lured more than one curious reader downtown. If not, the promise of visiting "the most tasty and attractive bakery and confectionery in the South" might have. Swedish immigrant Charles Lundberg built his bakery (at far right in the photograph) just four years after arriving in Austin as a journeyman baker. Modern city residents would envy Lundberg's commute to work, a one-block stroll from the house he and wife Annie shared at 10th Street and Colorado Street. To reach his business Lundberg passed the office of the five-year-old *Austin Democratic Statesman*. Founded in opposition to the Republican Reconstruction state government, the newspaper played a prominent role in that regime's defeat in 1873. Atop the rise at left sits First Baptist Church, built in 1856. Church legend tells of Sam Houston driving a peg into the ground across from the Governor's Mansion and proclaiming "I am a Baptist and right here we will build a Baptist church." Houston liked to whittle during services in the sanctuary, after which he often presented the small bobbin he had created to a fellow worshiper.

Congress Avenue at 10th Street, northwest corner
2004

In 1970 Governor Preston Smith complained, "I don't see why we have to save that old building. I'm told it isn't even the oldest building on Congress Avenue." Smith favored a developer's plan for constructing a state highway department office complex covering the entire block bounded by Congress Avenue, Colorado Street, 10th Street, and 11th Street. By then the Baptist Church had already found new downtown quarters and the site of the temporary Capitol adjacent to Lundberg's bakery lay covered in weeds and rubble. The bakery had barely escaped demolition in 1963 through a last-minute preservation effort by the Junior League and the Austin Heritage Society. Subsequently, the state bought the building, planning to incorporate it within the structure of the planned highway department complex. As preservationists aired their concerns and state legislators bickered, public support swung toward the bakery. Discovery of the temporary Capitol's foundation underneath the long-standing parking lot helped convince the Legislature *and* Governor Smith to locate the highway department elsewhere. In 1979 the State donated the Old Bakery and Emporium to the city of Austin.

Courtesy of Austin History Center, Austin Public Library C02589

14. Congress Avenue, looking south from the dome of the Capitol Building
1890s

Completion of the Capitol Building in 1888 offered Austinites an exhilarating view of their city. The 19th-century photographer had to lug heavy equipment up numerous dizzying spiral staircases to stand atop the Capitol dome. This photograph looking down Congress Avenue toward the Colorado River portrays a landscape of homogenous rooftops punctuated at intervals by more majestic structures, such as the Driskill Hotel in the distance at left (1) and the Travis County Courthouse in the immediate left foreground (2). Across Congress Avenue from the courthouse sits the temporary state Capitol (3), constructed hastily in 1882 after the original stone Capitol burned the previous year. The fledgling University of Texas held classes in this building from its inception until 1884. In the background the Colorado River flows eastward past the foot of Congress Avenue. Note the relative lack of development south of the river. The Texas State School For the Deaf and Dumb sits atop a hill surrounded primarily by farm land (4). Streetcar service did not extend across the river until construction of a concrete bridge in 1910. Until then residents were reluctant to buy land for houses in such a distant area intermittently isolated from the city by floods.

Congress Avenue, looking south from the dome of the Capitol Building
2004

Although many of the structures visible in the 19th-century photograph survive, modern skyscrapers now obscure most of them. The Driskill Hotel, still among the city's swankiest, lies across East 6th Street from the black office tower at 6th Street and Congress Avenue (just behind the "823"). Charles Lundberg's bakery on the northwest corner of Congress Avenue and 10th Street (arrow) is currently a giftshop run by the Junior League. The Travis County Courthouse was torn down in 1964 in favor of a parking lot. Trees block a view of the temporary Capitol's footings, which are preserved in a park-like setting.

Courtesy of Austin History Center, Austin Public Library PICA 01174

15. Southeast view from the dome of the Capitol Building
1890s

A young man snooping into shady dealings at the state land office disappears. Years later his decomposed remains are uncovered along the banks of a nearby creek. Is this the plot of the latest Hollywood thriller? Not by a long shot, for William Sydney Porter (O.Henry) penned his short story *Bexar Scrip No. 2692* when the land that became Tinsel Town still lay covered in orange groves. Porter set his story within the walls of the Gothic building in the foreground of this photograph. The General Land Office was built in 1858 on land originally set aside for the Governor's Mansion. That building's planning commission deemed the site too narrow, however, and land office employee Christoph Stremme drew up plans for his employer's new quarters in 1854. During Will Porter's stint in the land office between 1887 and 1891, he would have become well-acquainted with its cold, imposing interior and gloomy staircases. No better place for a tale of theft and murder!

Southeast view from the dome of the Capitol Building
2004

Somehow the General Land Office building survived when most other early government buildings did not. After the state land office moved to more spacious quarters in 1917, the Daughters of the Republic of Texas and the Texas Division of the Daughters of the Confederacy assumed control of the old building. The two organizations maintained separate museums on different floors. In 1970 the Gothic landmark was listed in the National Register of Historic Places. When the state legislature appropriated $4.5 million in 1989 for renovation, the museums located elsewhere and the building was converted into the Capitol Visitor's Center.

Courtesy of Austin History Center, Austin Public Library PICA 01136

16. Northeast view from the dome of the Capitol Building
1920s

A view northeast from the Capitol in the 1920s took in Texas Memorial Stadium (upper left), new home of the University of Texas football and track teams. Although the first football game in the $275,000 stadium took place November 9, 1924 (a 28-10 loss to Baylor), dedication ceremonies were held later in the month after the west stands were finally completed. Witnessing that first official game were 33,000 fans, at the time the largest crowd ever to attend a sporting event in Texas, as the Longhorns blanked arch-rival Texas A&M 7-0. A $125,000 expansion in 1926 added the horseshoe seating area on the stadium's north end and increased capacity by 13,500. At lower left, construction proceeds on St. Martin's Lutheran Church, completed in 1929. The new sanctuary replaced the original on 13th Street, which yielded to expansion of the Capitol's grounds. Note that the Capitol complex abuts a primarily residential neighborhood.

Northeast view from the dome of the Capitol Building
2004

A vastly different skyline now presents itself. The residential neighborhood has been replaced by a sea of government buildings in the foreground and an expanding University of Texas campus in the distance. Brazos Street at right is traversed by a connecting walkway of the Texas Employment Commission building and is completely interrupted by the Robert E. Johnson Building to the north (1). The renamed Darrell K. Royal-Texas Memorial Stadium (recognizing the popular football coach who brought two national championships to the school) is partially obscured by the LBJ Building (2). Having survived a demolition proposal by Board of Regents chairman William W. Heath in 1965, the oft-expanded stadium now seats over 80,000. A new track facility lies directly to the east. At far upper right is Disch-Faulk Field (3), home to the baseball team, while the Longhorn basketball teams play in the Frank Erwin Special Events Center (4) partially visible on Disch-Faulk's near side. Interstate Highway 35 slices across the city in the upper right, leading toward the white-roofed UT indoor football practice facility (5). The freeway replaced East Avenue in the 1950s and 1960s. St. Martin's Church fell victim to another Capitol grounds expansion in the 1950s. The small square structure in the left foreground (6) holds an elevator providing access to an underground Capitol office complex constructed in the 1990s.

Courtesy of Austin History Center, Austin Public Library PICA 01134

17. East view from the dome of the Capitol Building
1920s

From left to right East 14th Street, East 13th Street, and East 12th Street connect Brazos Street (foreground) with East Avenue. At the far end of 12th Street is the 15-acre campus of Samuel Huston College (arrow), named after an Iowa man who donated $9,000 to the school in its formative years. Initially conceived by the Methodist Episcopal Church in 1876, Huston College opened in the fall of 1900 with 80 African-American students. Six years later enrollment had reached 517. At about the time of this photograph the state department of education recognized Huston College as a class A senior college. At far left, where East 14th Street intersects East Avenue, City-County Hospital occupies the original block designated for this purpose by city planner Edwin Waller in 1839.

East view from the dome of the Capitol Building
2004

In 1952 Huston College merged with its East Austin neighbor Tillotson College and moved to Tillotson's campus on East 7th Street. A strip shopping center currently covers most of Huston's former campus. City-County Hospital, now called Brackenridge Hospital, has expanded well beyond its original allotment of land. As a regional referral center for much of central Texas, the medical complex includes a helicopter pad for its life-flight service. The Lorenzo de Zavala State Archives Building in the foreground dates to 1961. Its name honors the memory of the first vice-president of the Republic of Texas. Behind the archives building a garage provides parking for Capitol visitors. The wooded strip between the garage and hospital complex is Waterloo Park, established in 1978. Waller Creek, once the eastern edge of the city, flows through the park from left to right before emptying into Town Lake.

Courtesy of Austin History Center, Austin Public Library C01694

18. Colorado River, looking south from the foot of Brazos Street
c. 1869

Erratic service from Swisher's Ferry, the last of four ferry operators in the Austin vicinity, prompted citizens to build this pontoon bridge at the foot of Brazos Street in 1869. The *Daily Austin Republican* boasted, "No obstacles present themselves which have not been surmounted . . . the bridge itself. . . seems as solid as the everlasting hills." The *Austin Record* glowingly reported, "The bright and sparkling waters of the Colorado . . . seem to say; 'All hail to the invention of man . . . . Oh! beautiful City . . . when thou art decked with the splendor of coming years, I will murmur low and sing the requiem of the past.'" Alas, the "everlasting hills" proved sturdier. Within a year of its opening in November 1869, a 36-hour rain sent the bridge "glimmering to the Gulf."

Colorado River, looking south from the foot of Brazos Street
2004

A few years after losing the pontoon bridge, Austin spent $100,000 constructing a wooden bridge connecting the south bank of the Colorado with Congress Avenue. Subsequently the bridge collapsed under the weight of a herd of cattle, spilling dozens of the hapless animals into the water below. The International & Great Northern Railroad spanned the Colorado in the 1880s with the iron "Corporation Bridge" extending south from Congress Avenue. Riding a horse across the bridge cost 10 cents. A pedestrian paid a nickel. In 1886 the city of Austin bought the bridge and eliminated the unpopular toll. The current concrete bridge, visible in the upper right of this photograph, opened in 1910. Bridge expansion in 1980 inadvertently created an ideal habitat for the Mexican free-tailed bat. The "Bat Bridge" today is home to one of the largest urban bat colonies in the world.

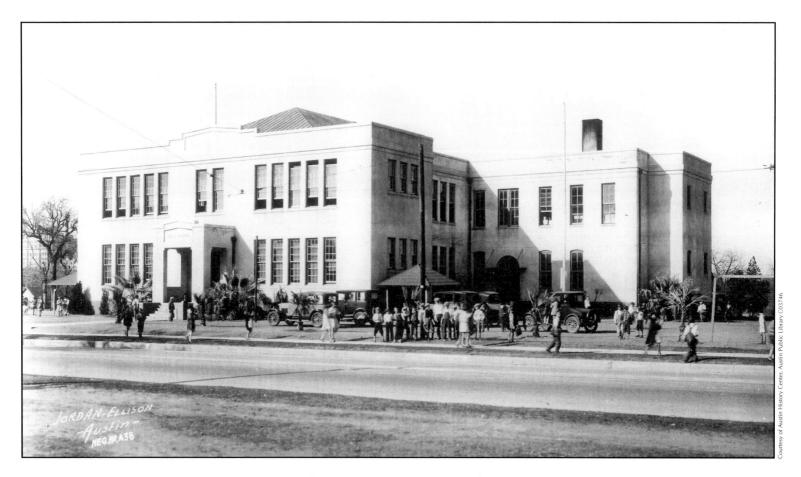

Courtesy of Austin History Center, Austin Public Library C03746

19. East 1st Street at East Avenue, northwest corner
1923

Austin's early Swedish presence is personified by Swante Palm, city resident for 49 years. Best remembered today as the donor of a vast book collection to the University of Texas, Palm also served as Travis County Justice of the Peace, Austin City Councilman, and city Postmaster. Beginning in 1866 he assisted Swedish immigration to Central Texas for 33 years as Vice Consul for Norway and Sweden. Three years after his death in 1899 the Austin school district renamed Tenth Ward Elementary School (see photograph) in his honor. This southeasternmost block in Edwin Waller's city plan originally held an arsenal. Owned first by the Republic of Texas, the facility became a federal installation after statehood in 1845. Austin accepted the land as a donation from the government in 1888. Four years later the city erected the Tenth Ward school building. Austin's first kindergarten began classes in Palm School in 1917. At the time of this photograph Palm School's enrollment of 637 students made it the largest elementary school in Austin.

East Cesar Chavez Street at Interstate Highway 35, northwest corner
2004

By 1976 Palm School had outlived its usefulness to the school district, resulting in its closure after 84 years of educating Austin children. Although the building's surroundings have changed considerably, its own appearance remains strikingly similar. Streetcar tracks no longer run along the former East 1st Street, now called Cesar Chavez. Interstate Highway 35 at far right replaced East Avenue in the 1960s. Two of the palm trees planted decades ago because of the school's name rise above the building's roof. At left are several Congress Avenue skyscrapers. Partially obscured by the taller palm tree is the new hotel for the Austin convention center. Palm School today houses the Travis County Human Services Department.

Courtesy of Austin History Center, Austin Public Library PICA 18809

20. East 1st Street, looking west at Red River Street
pre-1940

Gazing west along 1st Street in former times yielded a view of a wooded residential and small business downtown neighborhood. The construction crew in the foreground is working to bridge Waller Creek, the original eastern boundary of the city. This water barrier was a significant impediment to development east of town in Austin's earliest days. Once completed, the bridge in the photograph enabled streetcars to carry riders between Congress Avenue and east Austin.

Cesar Chavez Street, looking west at Red River Street
2004

Some of the trees remain, but houses have given way to gigantic structures such as the Austin Convention Center at right. At far left is the Four Seasons Hotel, marking the southern end of San Jacinto Boulevard as it terminates at Town Lake. The skyscraper in the distance stands at 100 Congress Avenue, the western extent of the old 1st Street streetcar. The Frost Bank Tower peeks over the Convention Center at right. Now bridged on every east-west street of Edwin Waller's original city plan, Waller Creek is easily overlooked by modern drivers. Carrying out a city plan to build a tunnel diverting flood waters from the creek would allow construction over a significant portion of the current flood plain. Rising cost estimates and inadequate funding may, however, kill the project.

Courtesy of Austin History Center, Austin Public Library PICA 15560

21. East 15th Street, looking west at East Avenue
1920s

In his original 1839 plan Edwin Waller allocated the far northeastern block of the city for use as a hospital. But not until July 1884 did Austin, sharing the $10,000 cost with Travis County, construct City-County Hospital on the site. The *Austin Daily Statesman* reported October 26, 1883 that "The new hospital . . . will be built with a view to the comfort of the unfortunates for whom its charity is intended." This first building is visible at right behind the newer version built in 1915. After the new building was completed local citizens began calling the facility "Brackenridge's Hospital," in recognition of Dr. Robert Brackenridge's role in convincing the city of its need. City Council officially changed the name to Brackenridge Hospital in 1929.

East 15th Street, looking west at Interstate Highway 35
2004

Even with the acquisition of several adjacent city blocks and demolition of its two original structures Brackenridge Hospital, the oldest operating public hospital in Texas, finds itself cramped for space. Interstate Highway 35 (the old East Avenue) blocks eastward expansion, while Waterloo Park to the west, the University of Texas' Frank Erwin Special Events Center to the north, and several commercial buildings to the south completely hem in the rest of the hospital complex. The newest incarnation of Brackenridge rises to the rear of the city's Children's Hospital (peaked roofs), which was constructed in 1988. The pediatric clinic building at left was added in 2001. Responding to tight finances Austin leased the entire facility to the non-profit Seton Healthcare Network in October 1995. Recognizing the need for more room Seton plans to build a new Children's Hospital farther north on land recently vacated when the city built a new airport. Brackenridge Hospital will utilize the vacated Children's Hospital, allowing Edwin Waller's hospital block to continue in its intended role.

Courtesy of Austin History Center, Austin Public Library PICA 00790

22. East 7th Street at East Avenue, northwest corner
1941

Austin's new City Market House at 7th Street and East Avenue replaced an informal gathering of produce sellers on this site when it opened June 6, 1935. Six hundred Travis County farmers attended that first day to sell their goods and compete for best-display prizes. As reported in the *Austin American*, a week's free stall rental lured producers "to permit them to become acquainted with the privileges afforded by the new market." Visitors arriving at the noon opening received free passes to Barton Springs.

The "negro boys band of the recreation department" provided a morning concert; at 3:30 the Austin Boys Band played. Later, the judging committee awarded prizes and former Mayor P. W. McFadden made a speech. Mayor Tom Miller then rose to "tell how the present administration accomplished the completion of the project." At the conclusion of the speechmaking, Austinites celebrated their new market house with an East Avenue street dance set to the amplified music of a square dance orchestra.

East 7th Street at Interstate Highway 35, northwest corner
2004

"City Market Kayoed by Supermarkets" announced a headline in the *Austin American* in February 1952. City Council in December 1951 cut off funds for "a public service for which there was practically no demand." The culprit was indeed the supermarket. Growers shifted to single crop farming and sold directly to this new type of grocery store; consumers responded to the convenience of shopping for so much variety under one roof. After demolishing the market, the city erected its first ever dedicated police headquarters building on the site. Describing the "swank" structure in March 1954 the *Austin Statesman* reported "it has comfort, beauty and utility, and most of all it has room." By the early 1970s, however, the department was cramped once again. An added second story failed to meet the need, and voters in 1979 approved bond sales to finance a new headquarters building on the site. Police Chief Frank Dyson commented, "We believe it will be one of the most sophisticated police buildings in the state." Today the expanded building also holds Austin's municipal court.

Courtesy of Austin History Center, Austin Public Library C00990

23. East 11th Street, looking west at East Avenue
1933

In the early 20th century East Avenue between the Colorado River and approximately 12th Street was known by local Spanish-speaking residents as "La Calle Ancha" (the wide street). This photograph, taken shortly after paving was completed in 1933, depicts one of the large center islands (parketas) which ran along much of the Avenue. The edifice at left was erected in 1894 as the East Austin School. The school district first acquired the property in 1883 and held classes in two small, yellow wood buildings. Children walked across one of two wooden foot bridges spanning Waller Creek to reach the school. Even in the subsequent, more permanent

structure, conditions at first were a bit primitive. The building had no running water until 1899, when fear of fire and the need to water newly-planted shade trees provided greater motivation than did student convenience. The school kept livestock, chickens, and dogs until 1901. In 1902 the district renamed the school for Jacob Bickler, a long-time Austin educator who had just died. German-born Bickler came to Austin in 1872 and taught Austin students for most of the next 30 years. He founded and directed the all-male Texas German and English Academy (1877-1887) and the co-educational Bickler Academy (1892-1902).

East 11th Street, looking west at Interstate Highway 35
2004

Construction of Interstate Highway 35 on top of East Avenue destroyed the parketas. A steady drone of humming automobiles and blasting 18-wheelers has replaced the earlier sounds of chatting neighbors, guitar players, and children playing baseball. The Bickler Building fell to a demolition crew in 1968. The school district had converted Bickler into an "opportunity school" for slow students in 1937 and an administration building in 1947. The building's cupola may still be seen as a gazebo in the Zilker Botanical Gardens. A chain hotel currently occupies the old school site.

Courtesy of Austin History Center, Austin Public Library PICA 05764

24. East Pine Street, looking east at Sabine Street
1871

On Christmas Day 1871 workmen laid the final rail completing the line between Houston and Austin. The *Austin Democratic Statesman* reported that "when the hammer had driven the last spike home, a yell arose from the multitude, and the joyous news flew to every part of the city . . . ." General Hamilton "spoke of the great era which had just been added to the history of our lovely city" which would "be looked upon as the herald of a glorious and progressive future." Many in the crowd admiring the "wonderful iron horse . . . had never seen such a thing before . . . after gazing and wondering, and uttering many strange and quaint remarks, they adjourned to their homes full of hopes for the future; smiling over the thoughts that everything hereafter should be cheaper and better, and that their home was now united with the rest of the world." That first engine was the Theodore Kosse, or Houston and Texas Central Railroad Engine #22. It arrived from Houston via East Pine Street. Here it lets off passengers at the Depot House on Waller Creek Bridge.

East 5th Street, looking east at Sabine Street
2004

By mid-twentieth century the "horseless carriage" had displaced the iron horse from its pre-eminent position in society. No clues remain at this intersection to remind one of that historic Christmas Day in 1871. As an exclamation point to this transition the concrete barrier dividing the city known as Interstate Highway 35 slices through the path of Austin's first railroad train. The high-rise hotel at left replaced a popular Mexican restaurant in the 1980s. The modern bridge spanning Waller Creek (lined by the larger trees to the right) is barely visible from this vantage point. This pedestrian most likely has little idea that he walks through the area of one of the most important events in the history of Austin.

Courtesy of Austin History Center, Austin Public Library PICA 03261

25. East 10th Street at Brazos Street, southeast corner
pre-1894

Early Austin Catholics, tired of relying on priests in distant Bastrop for religious direction, organized St. Patrick's Church under the Reverend Michael Sheehan at the corner of Ash (9th) Street and Brazos Street in 1853. Two years after assuming church leadership in 1864, the Reverend Nicholas Feltin changed the name to St. Mary of the Immaculate Conception. St. Mary's hired prominent Texas architect Nicholas Clayton in 1874 to design a new sanctuary. Clayton, whose later works included the main building of St. Edward's University in Austin, conceived the Decorated English Gothic structure in this photograph. Located one block north of the first church, the new building was consecrated one rainy April Sunday morning in 1884. Parishioner Michael Butler donated a 2,000 pound bell for the church's tower. Inscribed with the names of Butler's three children, the bell rang its first notes from the tower in 1886.

East 10th Street at Brazos Street, southeast corner
2004

Its appearance bolstered by the two asymmetric tower additions completed after 1894, St. Mary's remains an impressive downtown landmark. The Diocese of Austin named the church its cathedral in 1948. The entire complex includes St. Mary's Cathedral School, which offers pre-kindergarten through 8th grade classes. The school faces San Jacinto Boulevard and is partially visible at left in the photograph. No longer the tallest structure in its vicinity, St. Mary's Cathedral is topped from behind by Two Commodore Plaza.

Courtesy of Austin History Center, Austin Public Library C01165

26. East 7th Street at Brazos Street, northeast corner
post-1885

Parents seeking an education for their daughters in 19th-century Austin often turned to the institution in this photograph, St. Mary's Academy. The Holy Cross Sisters answered a call from St. Mary's Church in 1874 for help with operating a girls' parish school. The 1885 limestone building and grounds shown here occupied all of Edwin Waller's Block 85 (bounded by 7th Street, 8th Street, Brazos Street, and San Jacinto Boulevard). Waller built a two-story "mansion" for President Mirabeau Lamar on this block in 1839. After Lamar left office in 1841 the house quickly deteriorated and was destroyed by fire in March 1847. In the 1889-1890 Austin City Directory, the Holy Cross Sisters advertised that their academy "is located on one of the most beautiful sites in the city of Austin, so famous for its health and magnificent scenery." Of their building the Sisters claimed, "The Academy is one of the most imposing structures in the state, and its grand proportions are but indicative of the solid and sterling character of its internal advantages as a school."

East 7th Street at Brazos Street, northeast corner
2004

St. Mary's educated Austin's young girls from atop its hill in downtown Austin until 1947. That year the Sisters moved the school to the former E.H. Perry estate at East 41st Street and Red River Street. After admitting boys and changing its name to Holy Cross High School in 1968, the institution lasted only another four years before closing in 1972. The elegant downtown school building sat empty and unused until 1954. That year a demolition crew leveled not only the building, but also the hill upon which it sat. Since 1986 Austin Centre, a combined hotel and office tower, has occupied the site.

Courtesy of Austin History Center, Austin Public Library C00123

27. East Ash Street, north side between Congress Avenue and Brazos Street
1880s

Austin lumber merchant and city councilman Charles F. Millett opened the Millett Opera House (center) October 28, 1878, with "inimitable comedian" John Dillon starring in *The Comedy Event*. Reserved floor and balcony seats cost $1. A gallery ticket went for 50 cents. Designed by Frederick Ruffini, whose other works included the Texas School for the Deaf and the Old Main Building of the University of Texas, the building accommodated 800 people, or 7% of the city's population at the time. Only Galveston boasted a bigger Texas theater. John Phillip Sousa, Edwin Booth, Buffalo Bill Cody, William Jennings Bryan, and world-champion boxer Bob Fitz all made appearances. The Texas Legislature used the house occasionally while awaiting completion of the Capitol Building in 1888. Will Porter (O. Henry) was a regular patron and even appeared onstage with his wife in a production of *HMS Pinafore*. To the right in the photograph is the Millett Mansion, a residential boarding house built by Millett in the 1870s. For years the hotel was run by Mrs. S. J. Orr, called by the *Austin Statesman* "one of the best known hotel women in the state . . . Mrs. Orr's ability to properly look after the comforts of her guests is too well known to need further comment."

East 9th Street, north side between Congress Avenue and Brazos Street
2004

The 1898 opening of Hancock Opera House on West 6th Street lured patrons away from Austin's first proper opera venue. Converted initially into a skating rink and storage facility, Millet's building was purchased by the Knights of Columbus in 1911. The Austin Public Free Schools acquired the property in 1940 and by 1956 was prepared to demolish the former opera house. A long-term lease by a local printing firm then saved the structure and led to extensive interior restoration. In 1979 the school district leased Millet Opera House to its current tenant, The Austin Club, whose website invites citizens to "join this tradition of prestige and excellence." Next door, the last tenant left the Millett Mansion January 12, 1963. An *American-Statesman* headline blared "Mansion Doomed." The building, "solid as an Indian-fighting fort," with its two-foot stone walls, locally hand-made bricks, and solid walnut staircase, was destroyed for a parking lot. The skyscraper behind the parking garage now occupying the site is an office tower, Two Commodore Plaza.

Courtesy of Austin History Center, Austin Public Library PICA 28418

28. San Jacinto Boulevard, looking north at East Pecan Street
post-1870s

A solitary rider makes his way up an unpaved San Jacinto Boulevard towards Bois d'Arc Street and St. David's Episcopal Church. The two-year-old congregation of "The Church of the Epiphany" laid the cornerstone for this building April 7, 1853, across the street from the site of the short-lived, two-story presidential house of Mirabeau Lamar. Gothic towers and parapets were added to the building in the 1870s. Tension over the issues of slavery and states' rights briefly split the parish in 1856 when Charles Gillette led a small group of Northern sympathizers in the formation of Christ Church. At reunification in 1859, the two sides agreed to name their congregation The Church of St. David. Gillette again stirred controversy after secession in 1861 when he refused to read Bishop Alexander Gregg's prayer calling for "a speedy close to the unholy war forced upon us."

San Jacinto Boulevard, looking north at East 6th Street
2004

After the Civil War Bishop Gregg advised Texas Episcopal churches to rejoin the national church. In a pastoral prayer he urged worshipers to pray for Congress and the President. St. David's Church flourished throughout the rest of the 19th century. Prominent members included E.M. Pease, John Bremond, the Swisher family, and Peter Mansbendel. Charles Sumners, named rector of St. David's Church in 1939, was instrumental in founding St. Andrew's School and St. Stephen's School in Austin. In the early 1960s he led a successful resistance against efforts to move the church to a site near St. Andrew's. An expanding church eventually acquired the entire block between San Jacinto Boulevard and Trinity Street, which included the historic 1873 Castleman-Bull House. When the church later donated the structure to the Heritage Society of Austin, it also financed its relocation to Red River Street. St. David's stands today as the oldest church building in the city.

Courtesy of Austin History Center, Austin Public Library C00610

29. East 11th Street, looking west at Brazos Street
post-1876

Directly across from the Capitol once stood the medieval-looking Travis County Jail (left) and the ornate Travis County Courthouse (right). The smaller building adjacent to the prison housed the jailkeeper and his family. Austin's first prison, a log structure at West Cedar (4th) Street and Guadalupe Street, burned in the 1850s. The county then allocated $25,000 for construction of a stone jail and courthouse on the site. Men from a colony of Mormons near Mt. Bonnell (the colony having fled persecution in the north) were hired to erect the building in 1856. Citizens quickly realized that the site lay too far from the city center. The *Southern Intelligencer* reported in 1865 that "the juror who happens to be entitled to the promise of a dollar and a half from the county for services rendered, in which he has probably spent seventy-five cents worth of shoe leather, had to go out of town to get the slip of paper containing said promise." By 1875 other inadequacies became apparent. "The present jail is not only a disgrace . . . but a reflection upon civilization . . . it is a burning shame that thirty-four men should be crowded into a cell but fourteen feet square, there to inhale the foulest of atmosphere . . . in that stink-pen of iniquity and filth" (*Daily Democratic Statesman* Feb, 7, 1875). The Legislature eventually agreed, and the new facility in this photograph was completed in 1876.

East 11th Street, looking west at Brazos Street
2004

Perhaps the prison's most prominent resident was Will Porter in the late 1890s. Little known beyond Austin at the time, Porter subsequently gained famed with his short stories written under the pen name O.Henry. In the 1880s the jailhouse served temporarily as a state office building after fire destroyed the Capitol. Construction of a larger prison facility in 1933 doomed the anachronistic castle. The State Highway Department now stands in its stead. The Travis County Courthouse lasted a bit longer. It lost its usefulness as a court building with construction of the new courthouse and jail in the 1930s. The impressive towers were removed in 1931, which seemed fitting given the structure's new, more mundane function as an office building. In 1964 the historic landmark was leveled for a parking lot.

Courtesy of Austin History Center, Austin Public Library C03.206

30. West 11th Street at Colorado Street, looking northeast
c. 1907

Barely two decades old, the state's fourth Capitol Building serves as a backdrop to a line of mule-drawn wagons. Streetcar tracks and overhead wires offer evidence of the era's public transportation system. In 1881 a capitol planning board was working on plans for a new statehouse while meeting in the old stone Capitol Building when the structure caught fire and burned to the ground. The following February work began on a building designed by Elijah E. Myers, who also designed the Michigan and Colorado state capitols. When the newly-quarried limestone intended for the Texas building streaked with air exposure, builders switched to "Sunset Red" granite obtained near Marble Falls. Contractors imported stonecutters from Scotland to circumvent a boycott by the granite cutter's union, which was upset by the state's use of convict labor in the Marble Falls quarries. Finally, in April 1888 the new state Capitol opened with these words from Sam Houston's son Temple Houston, "This building fires the heart and excites reflections in the minds of all . . . the architecture of a civilization is its most enduring feature, and by this structure shall Texas transmit herself to posterity . . . ."

West 11th Street at Colorado Street, looking northeast
2004

A 1983 fire prompted formation of the State Preservation Board, which was tasked with protecting the beloved Capitol Building. After a major restoration project in the 1990s, the statehouse appears once again as it did in Temple Houston's day. To provide more space for the larger modern state government, workers excavated 65 feet of rock north of the building and built an underground office complex. Today the State Preservation Board is in its 21st year of fulfilling its mandate. The fountain and statue in the foreground comprise a memorial to Texans killed in World War II.

Courtesy of Austin History Center, Austin Public Library PICA 01114

31. Southwest view from the dome of the Capitol Building
1880s

On August 23, 1856, a large mob crowded into the building in the center foreground of this photograph to celebrate its opening as the new Texas Governor's Mansion. Governor Pease wrote his wife that the party was "a perfect jam. It is estimated that there were present at different times during the evening at least five hundred persons, and that over three hundred staid [sic] to supper." Built under the direction of Abner Cook, the dignified structure struck Pease as "a credit to the good taste of Texians." Across Colorado Street at lower left is First Baptist Church, serving a congregation organized in 1847 by Robert Hay Taliaferro. In 1880 the International and Great Northern Railroad built the bridge visible in the photograph spanning the Colorado River. Within a few years goods from the state's capital could be shipped by rail as far south as Laredo.

Southwest view from the dome of the Capitol Building
2004

Surrounded by skyscrapers, the mansion built by Abner Cook remains home to Texas' chief executive. First Baptist Church members worship across downtown in a sanctuary built in the 1960s. The site of its former home is now a parking lot. Trains still cross the Colorado River on the original railroad bridge, but the structure cannot be seen behind office buildings and apartment towers. Vegetation disguises the urbanized area south of the river, which appears to blend seamlessly with Zilker Park in the distance at right. At near right a cluster of trees marks the boundaries of Wooldridge Park. The low-slung building seen above the park is the Austin History Center.

Courtesy of Austin History Center, Austin Public Library C01139

32. West 1st Street, south side between Colorado Street and Lavaca Street
1935

Nearly seven decades ago the southern end of downtown Austin seemed remote enough for this fire department training tower. Built in 1931 for $6,200 the tower stands in isolation against a seemingly empty landscape. In fact, except for South Congress Avenue and its immediate environs, most of the land south of the Colorado River indeed lay undeveloped.

Periodic devastating floods (including one in the year of this photograph that came close to swamping the Congress Avenue bridge) deterred many who might otherwise have jumped at the chance of owning property so close to downtown. The Austin firefighters in this photograph have lined up along a narrow West 1st Street with the river at their backs.

West Cesar Chavez Street, south side between Colorado Street and Lavaca Street
2004

Austin firefighter James Buford died a hero when he drowned in a flooded Shoal Creek in 1972 attempting to save a 15-year-old boy. When the city spent $45,000 in 1978 restoring the 1st Street training tower, it chose to honor its fallen son by naming the edifice Buford Tower. The Italianate carillon was added during restoration. Four years earlier Mrs. Effie R. Kitchens, widow of the tower's builder, had donated $30,000 toward the project. Realizing that the downtown facility was no longer practical, the fire department had shifted its training program to a location far east of the city that same year. A much wider and busier 1st Street was renamed for Hispanic rights activist Cesar Chavez in 1993. Palmer Auditorium, a city landmark visible at left, will soon undergo a major transformation that will eliminate the distinctive checkered dome. The construction crane at right marks the site of a new city hall.

33a. West Hickory Street, looking west at Congress Avenue 1860s

Austin started here. On this spot in 1838 Texas Vice President Mirabeau Lamar shot and killed an enormous buffalo. Only a year later Lamar's friend Edwin Waller was hard at work converting the historic ravine into the main thoroughfare of the Republic's new capital city. A generation later the intersection had not progressed much beyond the appearance of a small-town crossroads. Atop the hill at right the Christian Church welcomed worshipers beginning in 1867. At upper left is the Shot Tower, so called because of local suspicion that its Unionist owner had allowed the manufacture of ammunition for Federal forces within it during the Civil War. Robert Alexander paid $250 for the lot in 1859 but it was his brother William who may have constructed the house in the 1860s. William Hamilton, Texas attorney general during Reconstruction, suffered distrust and ridicule from many of his secessionist Austin neighbors. An 1867 newspaper article described him thusly, "Cold and impassive, with no friendships that he holds sacred, he sits in his Shot Tower like a bottle-bellied

spider and weaves his web." But after his death in 1882, the Bar of Austin praised lawyer Hamilton's "amiable disposition, his love of right, his honesty in business affairs, his pure life, and his delicate sense of professional honor."

33b. West Hickory Street, looking west at Congress Avenue post-1905

Austin paved its first street in 1905 when it laid bricks over Congress Avenue. By that time this intersection appeared far more urban. In 1856 the Texas Legislature had granted the site of the first Capitol on the northeast corner of 8th Street and Colorado Street to the city for a new City Hall and Market House. Designed by Austin mayor and carpenter Leander Brown and constructed by Abner Cook in 1870, the ungainly edifice is mostly obscured in this photograph by Central Fire Station #1. The fire station was home to Colorado Fire Company #2, the third fire company in the city when it formed in 1871.

Courtesy of Austin History Center, Austin Public Library C00690

Courtesy of Austin History Center, Austin Public Library PICA 27163

West 8th Street, looking west at Congress Avenue
2004

Destruction of the Shot Tower in 1974 rankles local preservationists to this day. In 1962 the Texas State Historical Survey committee designated the unique house a Recorded Texas Historic Landmark. Three years later the Austin Heritage Society cited the building as worthy of preservation. The Austin Landmarks Commission delayed conferring historic status in 1974 in return for a promise by owner Capital National Bank that the building would not be demolished. On October 3rd the wrecking ball struck anyway. City protest briefly halted demolition, but it was too late. Already partially destroyed, the building could attract no buyer and was leveled shortly thereafter. Across the street, a more spacious City Hall replaced the original in 1907. Aaron Kruger, son of Ukrainian immigrant Sam Krugerman, followed in his father's footsteps when he opened Kruger's Jewelry Company (left) in 1939.

Courtesy of Austin History Center, Austin Public Library C01101

34. West 8th Street at Colorado Street, northeast corner
1920

Shortly after laying out Austin's original street grid in 1839 Edwin Waller hired 200 workmen to construct the city's first buildings. Laboring in that blistering summer heat well known to current Austinites, the men erected a one-story log house 60 by 115 feet on a hill at Colorado Street and West 8th Street. A visitor in the 1840s described this structure, the Republic's Capitol, as "the abode of bats, lizards, and stray cattle." Three years after the Legislature moved into the first domed Capitol in 1853, it passed an act reported by the *Texas State Gazette* as granting "the City of Austin a complete title to the Cemetery grounds—and also the site of the old Capitol, on condition of the city erecting in three years from the passage of the act a neat and commodious City Hall and Market House." Although late, the city lived up to its promise, constructing a plain brick building on the site in 1870. Serving as city hall, marketplace, opera house, and (briefly) fire station, the edifice lasted until 1907, when the three-story building in the photograph was raised. During construction workers took off the top of the hill so as to place City Hall's ground floor level with that of the adjacent Central Fire Station #1.

West 8th Street at Colorado Street, northeast corner
2004

On May 20, 1938 an *Austin Statesman* headline sneered "Austin Cornerstone Party Meets, Lays Big Rock Egg." At a cornerstone-laying ceremony Louis Page, a member of the team designing a new City Hall, had rejected the building's granite cornerstone as unworthy. Construction started anyway as the builders merely saved a spot for the stone as it became available. A simple ceremony four months later marked the laying of the new, more acceptable stone on top of that placed in 1907. For the 31-year-old city hall building was not demolished. Taking advantage of the old edifice's structural soundness, the 1938 plan called for cutting away the front part of the building, expanding the original footprint, and surrounding everything with an Art Deco shell. When finished, the larger City Hall encompassed the ground previously occupied by the demolished fire station. Austin currently is constructing its first dedicated City Hall on a site other than the hill at 8th and Colorado. The old municipal building will remain as home to a variety of city government offices.

Courtesy of Austin History Center, Austin Public Library C01918

35. West Ash Street, looking northeast toward Congress Avenue
1876

Livestock still roamed Austin's downtown streets when Swante Palm snapped this photograph in front of his house on West 9th Street. A native of Sweden, Palm aided Swedish immigration to Central Texas in his capacity as Swedish Vice-Consul from 1872 to 1899. Directly behind the cattle is William Randolph's store selling "dry goods, notions, boots and shoes." The building on the northeast corner of Congress Avenue and 9th Street was constructed by M. M. Long in the 1860s for use as a livery stable in support of his Austin-Lampasas stagecoach line. Long had moved to Austin from Bastrop, where in 1857 he promoted his business in the *Bastrop Advertiser* as follows:

"M. M. LONG, Bastrop, will keep at his livery stable a No. 1 pack of Hounds well-trained for catching runaway negroes. Terms: Use of Dogs per day in this county $7.50 For catching negro in this county $15.00 Use of Dogs per day out of this county $10.00 For catching negro out of this county $25.00"

Long opened the Austin Opera House on the second story of his Congress Avenue building in 1871. Patrons complaining of the smell of manure from below welcomed the company's move to Charles Millett's newly constructed "proper" opera house in 1878. Millett's edifice is seen with its peaked facade facing East 9th Street at far right.

West 9th Street, looking northeast toward Congress Avenue
2004

By the 1880s Miles Long had moved his livery south to 401 Congress. Jules Bornefeld operated the Palace Saloon and Billiard Parlor with Parole whiskey and Tony Faust beer in the former stable and opera house. Other 19th-century residents included the Golden Rule Saloon and the Statesman Publishing Company. In 1900 Oddfellows Hall and Horace Haldeman's tobacco store shared the premises. Five years later Spalding Drug Store moved in, staying 24 years before a name change to Capital Pharmacy. Capital Engraving Company occupied the top floor between 1916 and 1929. In 1939 Boswell Turner installed one of

the city's first air-conditioning systems to lure customers to his jewelry store. During the 25 year occupancy of Mr. and Mrs. Benjamin Goodfriend's clothing store, the building's stone exterior was covered with plaster. After the Goodfriends left, the building was restored to its original appearance. Today it is home to a law firm. Millett Opera House, now fronted with a projecting balcony, remains visible on the north side of 9th Street. Swante Palm's house suffered demolition many years ago. Liberty Bank, lined by parked cars rather than cattle, has replaced the old dry goods store.

Courtesy of Austin History Center, Austin Public Library C01325

36. West 12th Street at Lavaca Street, northeast corner
c. 1930

In 1840 a handful of Methodists assembled in a log house southwest of what is now Wooldridge Park to hear the new preacher, the Reverend John Haynie. The Mississippi Conference had appointed Haynie the preceding December to serve the Texas Mission's "Austin Circuit," which included the territory between Bastrop and the new state capital. The congregation constructed its first church building in 1847 on the northeast corner of Congress Avenue and Cedar (4th) Street, having purchased the lot for $26. After moving to a new building at Brazos Street and Mulberry (10th) Street in 1854, the church reached its peak 19th-century membership of 675 in 1892. The early name Central Church, South stemmed from a mid-century national split among Methodists related to slavery. This designation gave way to Tenth Street Church until 1902, when First Methodist Church became the official name. In 1928 First Methodist built the Renaissance Revival structure in this photograph at 1201 Lavaca Street at a cost of $200,000. Common to this architectural period was the Pantheon-inspired dome, in this case surrounded and accentuated by rows of impressive columns. The more famous Capitol dome stands in the background. Streetcar tracks on Lavaca Street date this photograph to the period before 1940.

West 12th Street at Lavaca Street, northeast corner
2004

Other than the growth of trees and loss of the streetcar tracks, little has changed in this view over the past several decades. First Methodist's congregation grew steadily to a peak of 3,546 in 1953, when suburban churches began drawing members away from downtown houses of worship. Nevertheless, First Methodist thrived. In 1946 the church completed mortgage payments on its building, paving the way for purchase of additional nearby property for expansion. Construction of a church library and education building, as well as the acquisition of the Oetting Building at 13th Street and Lavaca Street, gave evidence of the congregation's prosperity. First United Methodist celebrated its sesquicentennial in 1990 as one of the few remaining downtown churches in Austin. Fourteen years later, the Reverend John McMullen serves as the 38th pastor of the 164-year-old church.

37. West 15th Street at Lavaca Street, southeast corner
c. 1887

When blacksmith Joel Bennett and his wife Julia defaulted on a loan from real estate agent Eugene Bartholomew in 1881, Bartholomew assumed ownership of an empty lot on the southeast corner of Lavaca Street and West 15th Street. Later one of Austin's first City Council members, Bartholomew was a rarity among 19th-century Texas politicians, a popular Republican. In 1883 he spent $600 erecting a stone house on his new property. Bartholomew realized a nice profit in 1885 when he sold the site to Mrs. Fannie Wayland for $4,000. After extensive renovations, including the addition of three unusual towers, Fannie's husband John moved his grocery, grain, and provisions store onto the premises. An 1887 advertisement in the *Austin Daily Statesman* contained a sketch of the building appearing much as it does in this photograph. By 1900 the Waylands had moved to Robertson County and sold their Austin building to tenants John Kallgren and William Lindahl. These two worked together selling animal feed until 1917 when Kallgren bought out Lindahl's share. After Kallgren's death in 1923, R. W. Shipp purchased the land and building for $16,000.

West 15th Street at Lavaca Street, southeast corner
2004

Tulane graduate Shipp practiced medicine in the Scarbrough Building from 1911 until 1954. He and wife Madeline, of the prominent Robinson and Bremond families, leased their building at 15th and Lavaca to a number of different tenants over the years. At Mrs. Shipp's death in 1961, her will bequeathed the property to several of her brother's children and grandchildren. By the end of the decade the structure housed Capital Oyster Bar and The Checkered Flag. Threatened with demolition, the Bartholomew-Rosner Building was purchased by the Texas Osteopathic

Medical Association (TOMA) in 1995. Once convinced of the structure's historic value TOMA invested heavily in extensive restoration. The three outside towers were rebuilt, original interior limestone walls were exposed, two original fireplaces were discovered and restored, and portions of the original Bartholomew house were uncovered and incorporated into the new design. The sanded and polished original pine flooring now in use undoubtedly conveys a different atmosphere than in the days of the old feed and grain store.

Courtesy of Austin History Center, Austin Public Library C06049

38. West 10th Street at Guadalupe Street, looking southwest
1910

Austin owes much to Louisiana native Alexander Wooldridge. After moving to the city at the age of 25 in 1872, he became a long-time civic leader who helped organize a public school system, chaired the committee which successfully lobbied the Legislature to appoint Austin as home to the state university, sat on the university's Board of Regents for 12 years, and served as Austin mayor for ten years beginning in 1909. As mayor, Wooldridge supported many infrastructure improvement projects, including the creation of Austin's first city park. Edwin Waller's 1839 plan called for four symmetrically placed public squares in the new capital, one of which was the block depicted here. But 70 years later Austin still had no parks. The square

in this photograph had become a dumping ground. Several civic groups, including the Women's Federated Clubs, the Business League, and the newly formed City Council (with new mayor Wooldridge), stepped forward to reclaim the block and create Wooldridge Park. Opening ceremonies in June 1909 involved speeches, a children's chorus, and music by Besserer's Band. The park quickly became a favorite gathering place for Austin citizens. Regular summer band concerts entertained thousands. Politicians delivered stump speeches. Lovers strolled the grounds while parents frolicked with children on the grassy slopes. The new bandstand (constructed at a cost of $550) served as a centerpiece for many of these activities.

West 10th Street at Guadalupe Street, looking southwest
2004

Politicians have taken their speeches to other local venues, but Austin residents continue to enjoy summer band concerts at Wooldridge Park. The renovated bandstand plays host to a variety of other pursuits as well, ranging from Giant Chess to the annual O. Henry Pun-Off to camping by the homeless. Glimpsed through the trees at left is the Austin History Center, once the main city library. A multistory office building rises in the background as a reminder of the park's urban setting.

Courtesy of Austin History Center, Austin Public Library C02045

39. Guadalupe Street, looking north at West 9th Street
c. 1940

These workers are rewiring one of Austin's famed moonlight towers. Residents first thrilled to city-wide street lighting in 1874 when new gas lights inspired the nickname "City of Perpetual Moonlight." In the early 1890s, as construction of Austin's new dam and generating station neared completion, city leaders debated the costs of various methods of electrical street lighting. The Fort Wayne Electric Company of Fort Wayne, Indiana, offered to install thirty 150-foot tall iron light towers, as well as all necessary poles and wiring for street, commercial, and domestic needs, in exchange for $70,000 and the city's dam railroad (which would be of no use once the dam was finished). The company furthermore guaranteed that "the light from the six lamps on each tower would be sufficient to see the time with an ordinary watch on the darkest night within a circle 3000 feet in diameter." Austin quickly accepted, and by the end of 1894 some 31 towers stood ready for use (the additional tower having been acquired in a later trade with Fort Wayne Electric). Testing of city water pipes from the dam concluded successfully in early 1895, and the moonlight towers first cast their glow over the city May 6, 1895. The mayor's report of that year happily exclaimed that "it [the lighting] was enthusiastically greeted by the people to whom it belonged." At left in the photograph is Wooldridge Park, behind which is the new Travis County Courthouse.

Guadalupe Street, looking north at West 9th Street
2004

Seventeen of the original 31 towers survive. The rest fell victim to deterioration, collapse, or wayward buses and city utility trucks. Serious attempts at renovation and preservation began in the 1980s, and the landmarks are now listed on the National Register of Historic Places. One evening in June 1930 three young boys stood at the base of this tower at 9th Street and Guadalupe Street. Someone said "Anyone who hasn't climbed the tower by the time he is twelve is a sissy," prompting 11-year-old Jamie Fowler and his friend Johnson Wood to risk the ascent.

Jamie then gained instant fame when he survived a plunge from the top through the center of the structure, bouncing among the metal bars on his way down. At Brackenridge Hospital Jamie's mother told reporters, "His body is a mass of bruises and cuts . . . but the doctors say there isn't a bone broken." Fowler later became an Austin policeman. In a 1956 article in the *Austin American-Statesman,* he admitted being reluctant to discuss the incident with his two sons. "I hate for the boys to know I was so foolish."

Courtesy of Austin History Center, Austin Public Library PICA 19753

40. West 9th Street, south side between Guadalupe Street and San Antonio Street
c. 1905

On New Year's Day 1883 a "crowd of excitement hunting citizens rushed over to the Raymond Plateau, whence was seen issuing a dense volume of smoke. It was the African Methodist Episcopal church in flames." Standing to the immediate northeast was the Swede-Lutheran Church; ". . . a little scorching was all the damage it sustained." After the flames had died down one bystander, while observing the smoldering embers, noted, "There is a lot of good wood burning over there that could be saved." Perhaps reflecting contemporary racial attitudes (all Austin firefighters at that time were white) "one of the gallant firemen remarked, 'Let it burn; we are not saving wood now.'" The Metropolitan A. M. E. Church evolved in the early 1870s from a small group of worshipers gathering in Tempie Washington's house. By 1873 the congregation met in a rough-board whitewashed building on San Antonio Street. Ten years later, as described by the article in the *Austin Daily Statesman* quoted above, fire destroyed the flimsy wooden church. Although the congregation had already started construction of a new stone sanctuary, the building was unfinished, and the Reverend Abraham Grant began conducting services in Smith Opera House on West Sixth Street. Luck intervened when the Lutheran church moved and sold their old sanctuary to the A. M. E. for $900. By 1884 the new stone church was ready, and the congregation moved once again. In this photograph, the Reverand C.W. Abbington stands in front of Metropolitan A. M. E. Church. The old Lutheran Church is seen at left.

West 9th Street, south side between Guadalupe Street and San Antonio Street
2004

The Lutherans left West 9th Street for a new sanctuary at Congress Avenue and 16th Street. That 1883 building survives as the Texas Historical Commission Library. In 1926 Austin constructed its first library building on the site of the old Lutheran Church at West 9th Street and Guadalupe Street. Seven years later, after more than 60 years on the west side of town, the Metropolitan A. M. E. Church followed black migration to East Austin and sold its property on West 9th Street to the city for construction of a larger library. The original library building was moved to 1165 Angelina Street. It is now the George Washington Carver Museum and Cultural Center. The A. M. E. Church building was demolished. In this modern photograph the 1933 library building occupies all of West 9th Street between Guadalupe Street and San Antonio Street. Construction of yet another, larger main library building directly to the rear in 1979 resulted in the original's current use as the Austin History Center, source for most of the historic photographs in this book.

Courtesy of Austin History Center, Austin Public Library C02129

41. West 15th Street, looking east at West Avenue
1929

In 1929 the downtown business district did not yet extend north of the Capitol. Houses and churches dominate this view of 15th Street, itself still a broad, tree-lined avenue split by center esplanades. Only a few cars are present to break the monotony of the pavement. One of Austin's moonlight towers (1) stands ready to provide nocturnal illumination. To the right of this tower in the distance is the newly-built St. Martin's Lutheran Church (2) on East 14th Street. Swiss missionary Henry Merz organized the Deutsche Evangelische Lutherische St. Martin's Kirche in 1883, the 400th anniversary of Martin Luther's birth. The initial church building constructed in 1884 on East 13th Street fell victim to Capitol grounds expansion a few years before this photograph was taken.

West 15th Street, looking east at West Avenue
2004

Fifteenth Street's esplanades have yielded to the demands of the automobile. Only thin, unlandscaped strips of grass now separate the two-way traffic. A steady stream of cars reflects the street's function as a major crosstown artery between Mopac Expressway and Interstate Highway 35. The moonlight tower is one of 17 survivors from the original 31. Its lights are seen just above the roof line of the Texas Medical Association Building. In the 1950s Capitol grounds expansion once again forced St. Martin's Lutheran Church to move. Three years after selling its land to the state in 1957, the congregation erected a new facility at 606 West 15th Street (seen at left with rounded roof and cross-mounted spire). Not many 15th Street residences remain. Between West Avenue and Interstate Highway 35 almost all have been replaced by office towers and government buildings.

Courtesy of Austin History Center, Austin Public Library C01955

42. West 6th Street, looking west at Congress Avenue
1920s

Several notable structures appear in this view from the top floor of the Scarbrough Building at Sixth Street and Congress Avenue. In the distance is the Alamo Hotel (1), which offered rooms for short-term visits or long-term residential leases. An undated menu from the hotel diner boasts of "80 rooms all bath" in the "fireproof" building with "Rates $2.50 down." A breakfast of "Brains & Eggs" sold for 40 cents while "Broiled T Bone Steak, hot biscuits or hot rolls and coffee" cost a dime more. Stately columns and an American flag on its roof mark the United States Post Office building (2). At far right, with its curved archways, is the Federal Courthouse (3), which doubled as a post office before construction of its successor two blocks west. The 1881 building was the first permanent home of the postal service in the city. In 1898 Will Porter, later known as O. Henry, was convicted of bank embezzlement in this building.

West 6th Street, looking west at Congress Avenue
2004

By the end of its life the Alamo Hotel was known for its cheap lodging, shady characters, and downstairs music lounge. Sam Houston Johnson, brother of Lyndon, lived on the top floor until his death in the 1970s. The Alamo Lounge hosted poetry readings and live musical acts, including Tom Waitts, Townes van Zandt, Jimmie Dale Gilmore, and Butch Hancock. Austin lost one of its funky landmarks when the building was razed in 1984. Homeless advocate Brother Tony Hearn, angry at the hotel's impending demolition, publicly cursed the site by sprinkling animal blood around its perimeter. Within a few years the lot's owner, Lamar Savings & Loan, had gone out of business while Lamar's president, who had ordered the building's destruction, had been convicted of business fraud. The University of Texas now owns both the old Post Office and the Federal Courthouse. The former has been renamed Claudia Taylor Johnson Hall in honor of the one-time first lady. The site of O. Henry's trial is now known as O. Henry Hall.

Courtesy of Austin History Center, Austin Public Library PICA 02690

43. West 6th Street at Rio Grande Street, northeast corner
post-1906

In 1890 19-year-old Henry Maerki emigrated to America from Windisch, Switzerland, on $60 borrowed from his sister. Arriving in Austin with 50 cents in his pocket, he quickly found work in Charles Lundberg's bakery on Congress Avenue. Back home Maerki had apprenticed in both bread- and cake-making, two distinct trades in Europe at the time. After Lundberg's death in 1895, Maerki and Frenchman J. Jaccard purchased the business, but within a short time Maerki was sole owner. Beginning in 1896 Henry tended the oven and baked the bread while new bride Lillie ran the store. The couple sold the business in 1906 and toured Europe, where Henry gathered recipes and learned new techniques. Back in Austin Maerki erected the frame building at left in this photograph to house his new bakery at West Sixth Street and Rio Grande Street. Keeping up with the times, the Swiss baker later installed modern bread-making machines in a newer brick building (center). A contemporary newspaper article described the bakery's oil-fueled Duhrkop oven as capable of baking 10,000 loaves of bread a day. Besides increased production, Maerki appreciated that "I don't have to rush out every now and then for wood as I did in the early days."

West 6th Street at Rio Grande Street, northeast corner
2004

As most Austinites now buy their bread in grocery stores, not many family-owned bakeries remain in the city. Even so, Maerki's original brick building still stands at the corner of West Sixth and Rio Grande Streets. The frame structure came down for expansion of the brick edifice, current home to Katz's Deli and Bar (ground floor) and Momo's Club (upper floor). New Yorker Marc Katz left his native city in 1977 for greener pastures in Texas. After two years as a car salesman Katz, with his friend Abe Zimmerman, purchased the old bakery for use as a restaurant and deli. Now sole owner, Marc Katz has become locally famous in television commercials for his 24-hour eatery in which he exclaims, "I can't help it, I gotta tell ya, Katz's never closes!"

Courtesy of Austin History Center, Austin Public Library PICA 02009

44. West 6th Street, looking east at Guadalupe Street
1940

Almost three decades after opening, Austin's two original skyscrapers, the Littlefield Building on the left and the Scarbrough Building on the right, remained the tallest structures on 6th Street. An appliance store, shoe repair shop, cafe, and other small businesses give evidence in this photograph of a thriving commercial district along West 6th as it approaches Congress Avenue. Flying an American flag atop its roof at left is the Federal Post Office. One block farther east of the Post Office is O. Henry Hall, the federal courthouse in which Will Porter (O. Henry) was convicted of bank embezzlement.

West 6th Street, looking east at Guadalupe Street
2004

Both the Scarbrough and Littlefield buildings are now dwarfed by younger giants. The Littlefield Building is barely visible behind One America Center while the Scarbrough Building is sandwiched between Bank of America Center (1) and Bank One (2). The 300 West Sixth Street Building at far left lends a cavernous quality to the scene. In this building's shadow is the Post Office (now Claudia Taylor Johnson Hall) while O. Henry Hall is hidden by the trees at the base of One America Center. At far right is the Frost Bank Tower.

Courtesy of Austin History Center, Austin Public Library PICA 05976

45. West 6th Street at Colorado Street, northwest corner
1890

Before air-conditioning and electric refrigerators, the appeal of a cool drink on a sweltering Austin summer day must have been a strong one. Henry Petri's Phoenix Saloon slaked many a 19th-century thirst in the Texas capital with its "ice cold lager beer." In an 1889 advertisement, then-proprietor John Kempe boasted that patrons could also enjoy "wines and liquors of the finest brands," "the finest imported and domestic cigars," and a "fine hot lunch served every day." A newspaper clipping of the era reported that "something good to cheer the drooping spirits is always to be appreciated, and John Kempe, of the Phoenix Saloon, is the man to supply your wants."

West 6th Street at Colorado Street, northwest corner
2004

Today only water flows on the premises. In place of the Phoenix Saloon is a tree-lined plaza situated at the entrance to the University of Texas' Claudia Taylor Johnson Hall. Erected as a United States Post Office in 1912-1914, the building was impressive enough at the time to appear on post cards sold to tourists. A new edifice in 1965 motivated the federal government to donate the structure to UT. After extensive remodeling, Johnson Hall (in honor of the wife of former president Lyndon Johnson), opened for university administration use in 1970. Phoenix Saloon owner Henry Petri is not entirely forgotten in today's Austin; his name remains chiseled into the 1907 City Hall cornerstone two blocks north.

Courtesy of Austin History Center, Austin Public Library PICA 05041

46. East 6th Street at Brazos Street, northwest corner
c. 1890

Austin residents welcomed construction of the luxurious Driskill Hotel in 1886. Lucky guests could choose from 60 steam-heated rooms and four large second-story suites. An elegant skylit restaurant provided patrons with the finest dining experience in Austin. Male guests found diversion in the billiard room, bar, and barbershop, while women and children entertained themselves in special rooms set aside for them. Tennessee native Colonel Jesse Driskill arrived in Texas by way of Missouri in 1849. He made and then lost a fortune selling cattle to the Confederacy during the Civil War. Driskill moved to Austin in 1869 and began re-accumulating his herds. Once again a wealthy cattle baron by the 1880s, he purchased the lot bordered by 6th, 7th, and Brazos streets in 1884 for $7,500. A severe drought and unusually cold weather in 1888 killed 3,000 of Colonel Driskill's cattle, wiping out his fortune once more. Driskill sold his namesake hotel shortly thereafter.

East 6th Street at Brazos Street, northwest corner
2004

Notable among subsequent owners is George Littlefield, builder of one of the first skyscrapers in Austin adjacent to the Driskill Hotel. A 12-story Driskill hotel annex bordering 7th Street was added in 1930. Four years later a young, boisterous politician invited the shy Claudia Taylor to breakfast at the Driskill. In 1964 Lyndon and Ladybird Johnson returned to the site of that first date to await election results for LBJ's successful presidential bid. By 1969 the Driskill Hotel was near bankruptcy. Demolition seemed imminent. A successful fund-raising drive by the Austin Heritage Society saved the historic structure. The hotel re-opened amid much celebration in 1973. Today, the once-again elegant Driskill Hotel anchors the western end of historic East 6th Street. Busts of Colonel Driskill and his sons continue to look down from their perches atop the south, east, and west facades, as they have for the past 118 years.

Center for American History, UT-Austin CN Number 11881

47. East 6th Street, looking west toward San Jacinto Boulevard
1888

East 6th Street in 1888 was the busiest shopping thoroughfare in the city. Business prospered along the route of the streetcar line connecting east and west Austin. Originally populated by cruder wooden buildings, East 6th Street underwent a construction boom in the 1870s in which a number of magnificent stone and brick edifices appeared. Towering at the far end of the street at its intersection with Brazos Street is the Driskill Hotel (1886). Closer in is Joseph Hannig's widely admired Renaissance Revival building, erected in 1876 for Hannig's cabinet and undertaking enterprises. Hannig's wife at the time of construction was Alamo survivor Susanna Dickenson. After his wife's death in 1883 Hannig moved to San Antonio. In 1888 the

building held Morley Brothers pharmacy. A report in the Austin city directory claimed that the brothers' products "represent the very *acme* of excellence and efficacy." Daniel Weaver operated a grocery store in the two-story building on the northeast corner of 6th Street and San Jacinto Boulevard. On the other side of 6th, a projecting sign advertises H. T. and C. W. Kluge's saddle and harness business. Establishing their concern in 1886, the brothers were "prepared to promptly and efficiently do anything in their line at reasonable prices." Following the pattern of many 19th-century commercial districts, East 6th Street buildings in 1888 offered upper-story residential housing.

East 6th Street, looking west toward San Jacinto Boulevard
2004

Construction of the new Capitol in 1888 initiated a shift of commercial activity away from East 6th Street and toward Congress Avenue. By the middle of the 20th century the one-time bustling thoroughfare had deteriorated into a row of crumbling buildings and seedy businesses. Designation of a nine-block stretch of the street as a National Register District in the 1960s planted the seeds of recovery, and by the 1970s East 6th was alive once more because of the attractions provided by numerous live-music venues. Almost all of the buildings in the 1888 photograph remain. Where once dry goods stores, millineries and wagon shops drew local residents in search of basic supplies, East 6th now appeals to locals and tourists alike with its many restaurants, nightclubs, and comedy clubs. A typical weekend night finds dozens of bands playing for thousands of visitors to the district. In the brick building only partially visible at far right is Pecan Street Cafe. Opening in 1972, the restaurant was an early pioneer of 6th Street restoration and is now one of the oldest businesses along the historic street.

II. East Austin

East Avenue and Beyond

"... all the facilities and conveniences be provided the Negroes in this district [east Austin], as an incentive to draw the Negro population to this area."
— 1928 Master Plan, City of Austin

East Austin's history is to a large degree the story of race relations in the state capital. Through the years the area has been home to more different ethnic enclaves than just about any other part of town. Italian, Swedish, German, and Irish immigrants have all called East Austin home. More recently city government intentionally concentrated African-American and Hispanic populations on the far side of East Avenue. Although such blatant forms of racism are now illegal, many of today's East Austin residents feel that subtler forms of discrimination continue to harm their neighborhoods.

Waller Creek was the original divider of east from west. As bridges began spanning the waterway, East Avenue assumed that role, aided by a natural rise running north from 7th Street. The arrival of rail service to the city in 1871 brought with it the need for a large freight-handling area. Vital but inherently unattractive facilities developed along 4th and 5th streets in the east.

After the Civil War former slaves established multiple African-American communities around Austin. As Austin expanded, these areas were annexed by the city, and white residents coveted what was now valuable real estate. Responding to this pressure, blacks began moving east in increasingly large numbers. The relocation of several black churches to East Austin expedited the migration.

Mexican-Americans initially arrived in Austin as a community of laborers in the 1850s. Early white citizens disliked and distrusted Hispanics. Fear of escaped or rebellious slaves found release as anger directed at the Mexican-Americans accused of encouraging them. In 1854

Austin mayor Rip Ford led a "Vigilance Committee" on a march to the encampment of Mexican-Americans to issue an ultimatum. The Mexicans must leave or be forcibly evicted. Most left.

A later Mexican-American community fared better. Beginning about 1870 a large Hispanic neighborhood developed in Austin's manufacturing zone around lower Guadalupe Street. In 1907 the community founded the first Hispanic church in the city when it built Our Lady of Guadalupe Catholic Church at the intersection of 5th Street and Guadalupe Street. The arrival in the 1920s of Walker's Austex Chili Factory, an early pioneer of mainstream Tex-Mex food, provided jobs for many neighborhood residents.

A 1919 incident illustrates contemporary attitudes behind the racist municipal policy appearing so blatantly in 1928. On the street in front of the Driskill Hotel white NAACP worker John Shilladay was publicly beaten by a group which included County Judge Dave Pickle. Pickle defended the attack with the claim that Shilladay received "a good thrashing on general principles." The assault victim left town under police escort. Texas Governor William Hobby offered public support for Judge Pickle, citing Shilladay as the "only offender."

Austin's 1928 city plan called for establishment of a "Negro district" east of East Avenue. The city would withhold services from any black neighborhood outside of East Austin. African-Americans were banned from all city recreational facilities except for Rosewood Park in the east. Mexican-Americans received similar treatment. Our Lady of Guadalupe Church moved east under pressure, while the city

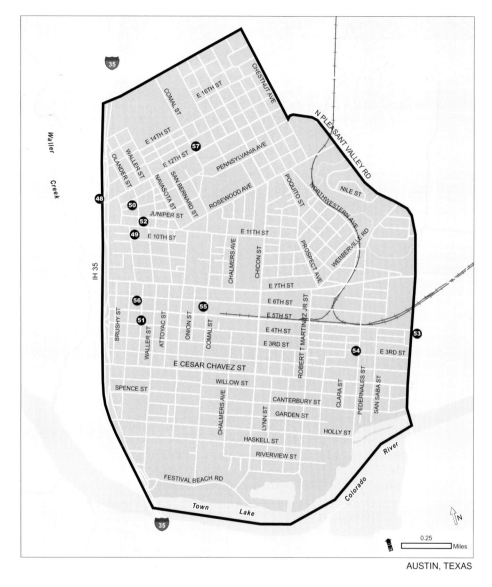

AUSTIN, TEXAS

Mexican identity. East 11th Street developed into an unofficial dividing line between Hispanics to the south and blacks to the north. When in the 1930s Congressman Lyndon Johnson and Mayor Tom Miller brought construction of the first public housing units in the country to Austin, three separate facilities were built. Against Johnson's wishes one unit each was designated for Anglos, African-Americans, and Mexicans, with each located in the appropriate East Austin neighborhood.

Interstate highway construction in the 1950s added an imposing physical barrier between east and west to the psychological barrier already in place. A graceful, landscaped East Avenue was destroyed for a rising wall of pavement slicing from south to north. Behind this wall, lax city zoning policies contributed to the area's seedy appearance as junk yards and manufacturing plants intermingled with peoples' homes. City neglect resulted in rundown schools, broken or unpaved streets, increased pollution, and overgrown parks.

Austin remains a racially divided city. East Austin remains home to most of the city's African-American and Hispanic population. Many are optimistic for a better future, however, as official government policy transitions from hostility to tolerance to reconciliation. Recently, some in city government even proposed renovating and beautifying the land underneath the elevated Interstate Highway 35 in an attempt to lessen its divisive visual impact.

With support from the city, East Austin residents in recent years have worked hard to improve the area's appeal. City policies now aim to redevelop 11th and 12th street corridors with a healthier mix of small businesses, community centers, and affordable housing. These efforts occasionally run counter to the goals of historic preservationists. The story of the Buratti Building on East 6th Street vividly highlights such conflict. Thus, through renewal or replacement, the East Austin of tomorrow will contrast greatly with the East Austin of yesterday and today.

Recreation Department opened Zaragosa Park as "the Community Center for all the Mexicans of Austin."

These policies had the desired effect. Of the black communities, all but Clarksville gradually vanished. The area around "Chili Square" lost its

Courtesy of Austin History Center, Austin Public Library C02070

48. East Avenue, looking south at East 12th Street
1930

East Avenue at one time offered broad traffic islands with park-like landscaping to soften the effects of urbanization on the city. The islands served as gathering places for family picnics, neighborhood discussions, and impromptu musical performances. At left is the campus of Samuel Huston College, one of the few institutions in the south providing college-level instruction for blacks. Jackie Robinson, who later gained fame as the first African-American to play baseball in the National League, once coached the Huston College basketball team. The cupola at right graces the Bickler Academy, one of the first public schools in Austin when it opened in 1894. St. Edward's College is visible in the distance (arrow).

Interstate Highway 35, looking south at East 12th Street
2004

Construction of Interstate Highway 35 in the 1950s and 1960s dramatically altered both the appearance and function of old East Avenue. Without the inviting traffic islands the current highway holds no appeal to pedestrians. Widening of the roadway displaced many homes and neighborhood businesses, thereby opening the door to the gas stations and hotels now lining the corridor. When Huston College and Tillotson College merged in 1953, the former institution abandoned its East Avenue campus for that of Tillotson on East 7th Street. A strip shopping center replaced Huston's academic buildings and residential dormitories. The Bickler Academy was torn down in 1968 to accommodate the Marriott Hotel, although its cupola survives in Zilker Park. The always crowded Interstate Highway 35 is a major commercial link between Mexico and large American markets to the north.

Courtesy of Austin History Center, Austin Public Library PICA 04046

49. East 10th Street, north side between San Marcos Street and Waller Street
1950s

The Reverend C. Ward founded the Third Baptist Congregation on East 10th Street in 1875. Completion of a brick sanctuary in 1885 inspired the name Ebenezer Baptist Church, "Ebenezer" meaning "stone of help." The present Gothic Revival structure first saw service in 1955. One of its towers houses the bell from the first brick church. That same year, Ebenezer and 19th Street Baptist churches of Austin were accepted into the Austin Baptist Association as well as the Baptist General Convention of Texas and the Southern Baptist Convention, thereby breaking the BGCT color barrier.

East 10th Street, north side between San Marcos Street and Waller Street
2004

One hundred twenty-nine years after its founding Ebenezer Baptist Church remains a strong force in the East Austin community. Church leaders have been closely involved with recent efforts at revitalizing the area. Ebenezer's main building has changed little over the past 50 years. The yards and driveways of houses across East 10th Street from the church attest to the persistent residential character of the neighborhood. This west-facing view provides a rare distant glimpse of the Capitol, a landmark which once dominated the landscape from all approaches to the city but which is now largely hidden by downtown skyscrapers.

Courtesy of Austin History Center, Austin Public Library PICA 20860

50. Olive Street at Curve Street, northwest corner
c. 1907

Until 1889 there was no high school for African-American children in Austin. That year the Austin Colored High School, later known as Robertson Hill School, opened at San Marcos Street and East 11th Street. In 1907 the school moved into the wood building pictured here. With the move came a name change to Anderson High School, after E. H. Anderson, former president of Prairie View Normal School (now Prairie View A&M University). Anderson was born of slave parents in 1850 Tennessee. After graduating from Fisk University, he moved to Texas in 1879 to head Prairie View, which at the time was intended primarily to train black teachers. Anderson's brother L. C. succeeded him as president upon his death in 1885.

Olive Street at Curve Street, northwest corner
2004

L. C. Anderson moved to Austin to become principal of Robertson Hill School in 1896. Thus, he oversaw the school's transition from Robertson Hill to his brother's namesake school in 1907, as well as the move to a larger, more permanent structure elsewhere in East Austin in 1913. Anderson administered the school and taught Latin until illness forced his retirement in 1928. Subsequently the campus was renamed in his honor.

The city closed the school in 1971 in response to federally imposed integration orders. The school building at Olive Street and Curve Street was razed years ago. A park since 1953, the site was acquired from the school district by the city parks department in 1978. At left, Brackenridge Hospital peeks over the trees from the one-time northeast corner of the city at East 15th Street and Interstate Highway 35 (formerly East Avenue).

Courtesy of Austin History Center, Austin Public Library PICA 27198

51. San Marcos Street, looking north at East 4th Street
1911

Much that was vital to Austin's early prosperity passed through this rail freight yard on the east side of town. The Houston and Texas Central Railroad was the first to reach Austin when it completed its line from Houston in 1871. The Austin and Northwestern Rail Road was formed in 1881 to connect Austin with towns to the northwest. Its founders included several prominent Austin businessmen and civic leaders, including Walter Tips, A. P. Wooldridge, William Brueggerhoff, and J. J. Tobin. By the time of this photograph, the Southern Pacific had acquired both of these railroads.

San Marcos Street, looking north at East 4th Street
2004

By the 1970s, the Southern Pacific had lost interest in its 167-mile Houston-Austin line and was allowing the tracks to deteriorate. The City of Austin purchased Southern Pacific lines running through the city in 1986 to preserve the tracks for later use in a mass transit system. Eighteen years later the city is still without street rail transportation. When the tracks running across downtown were closed, those in this photograph became obsolete. Austin's original rail freight yard today is little more than an empty, neglected field.

Courtesy of Austin History Center, Austin Public Library PICA 02684

52. East 11th Street, north side between Curve Street and Waller Street
c. 1907

German immigrant Richard Arnold (arrow) holds his granddaughter while posing with members of his family in front of his East Austin bakery in 1907. Arnold originally worked in Charles Lundberg's New Orleans Bakery at 10th Street and Congress Avenue. After two years spent running his own bake shop on East 6th Street, Arnold moved his business into this building in 1891. The baker and his family lived over his shop in the wooden building at right. Standing on the porch at far right is Lillie Maerki, wife of another prominent Austin baker, Henry Maerki. Her daughter Nina Mae is the smaller of the two children seated on the horse nearest to Lillie.

East 11th Street, north side between Curve Street and Waller Street
2004

After 1922 Arnold Bakery was passed on to relatives of its founder and renamed Reuter's Bakery. Jimmie and Georgia Owens bought the place in 1946 and converted it the following year into the Southern Dinette, which quickly acquired the reputation of serving the best soul food in East Austin. The diner thrived on a bustling East 11th Street during the heyday of the "Chitlin Circuit," a national collection of venues available to black musicians during the Jim Crow era. Most famous of these in Austin was the nearby Victory Grill, still in operation a block to the east. After Jimmie died in 1976, wife Georgia kept the eatery going another twelve years. By then the neighborhood had deteriorated into an area of crime, drugs, and prostitution. The eastern half of the building burned in 1990. Within a few years demolition threatened the by-now-abandoned western remnant. The Austin Revitalization Authority purchased the historic landmark in 2000, selling it in 2001 to Shoehorn Design with the stipulation that the building be preserved and renovated. Next to the restored Arnold Bakery Building rises the Snell Building, another component of East Austin's revival.

Courtesy of Austin History Center, Austin Public Library PICA 00607

53. East 5th Street at Pleasant Valley Road, southeast corner
1939

In 1913 Austin Mayor Alexander Wooldridge proposed allocating $50,000 for the construction of a municipal abattoir. Evidently Wooldridge's plea was ignored, for in August 1929 the *Austin American-Statesman,* in an article on spending from a recently approved bond fund, reported "It is almost a definite certainty that the new $75,000 abattoir will be built in 1930." When the slaughterhouse finally opened in April 1931, Austinites could take their animals to "be killed at the Abattoir under City inspection and sanitary regulations" with "a complete inspection [by] a qualified Veterinarian. . . made on the killing floor." A 1937 *American-Statesman* report noted that Austin's abattoir was "the largest such municipal plant in the United States."

East 5th Street at Pleasant Valley Road, southeast corner
2004

By 1943 the federal government was endeavoring to force the closing of Austin's abattoir. A newspaper reporter lamented that "closing the abattoir would send the state back to the primitive procedure of butchering its meat out under the trees." In the early 1960s the city leased the facility to Austin Community Livestock Processors, which in turn terminated the agreement in 1969 due to "high financial losses." In April of that year the Austin City Council "unhappily accepted the closing of the city's only slaughterhouse." The building was razed shortly thereafter. Employees of Capital Metro, which now occupies the site, speak of eerie late night noises and apparitions, perhaps providing lingering evidence of the area's gorier past.

Courtesy of Austin History Center, Austin Public Library PICA 02722

54. Santa Rita Street, looking west at Pedernales Street
1940

Is it any surprise that Congressman Lyndon Johnson was able to grab the first piece of the new state housing authority funding pie for his constituents? When the federal Housing Act of 1937 ordered the states to organize public housing agencies, Texas Governor James Allred responded by convincing the Legislature to pass the only public housing act in the state's history. Congressman Johnson then enlisted the support of Austin Mayor Tom Miller in diverting the initial cash flow to his district. The first of three Austin units opened in 1939. At the insistence of local white authorities, the Santa Rita project in this photograph was designated for Mexican-American residents only.

Chalmers Court would house whites, while Rosewood would be set aside for African-Americans. An article in the *Austin Statesman* written three months after Santa Rita's opening lauded the pride residents displayed in their new home. "Peep in the front doors and you view humble efforts at decorations, bright paper flowers, little ornaments . . . maybe a china dog (slightly chipped) . . . and the inevitable colored print of the Madonna and Christ Child." Furthermore, "on top of every spotless, white porcelain kitchen stove in Santa Rita is a pot of brown beans bubbling under a low flame. Whether it is a lean-to shack or a modern housing unit-this means it's home to these Mexican families."

Santa Rita Street, looking west at Pedernales Street
2004

In June 1996 auditors from the U. S. Department of Housing and Urban Development issued a scathing report after visiting the country's oldest public housing project. Broken windows, graffiti, and clogged toilets plagued some of the 97 Santa Rita apartments, 21 of which were vacant. Through the efforts of new Executive Director Jim Hargrove the complex rehabilitated itself. By 2001 HUD was citing Austin's housing authority as an example for others to follow. Santa Rita today houses a more diverse population than in the past. Although troubled with the same problems of crime and drugs affecting housing projects throughout the nation, the country's first and oldest project continues to serve Austin's low-income residents.

Courtesy of Austin History Center, Austin Public Library C05417

55. East 6th Street at Comal Street, southwest corner
1936

J. B. Pierce and his brother opened their East Austin meat market in this sturdy-looking brick building in 1914. Customers with telephones dialed 988 to reach the shop, from which the brothers offered "choice beef, pork, mutton, veal, lard, and sausage." Perhaps anticipating the large chain grocery stores which would eventually drive most small markets from the scene, the Austin Packing Company in 1936 advertises its status as a "home enterprise."

East 6th Street at Comal Street, southwest corner
2004

Rudy Cisneros began selling buttermilk biscuits, Mexican pastries, and coffee from the former meat market in the 1950s. Unlike his baker father, who had run the popular Sunset Bakery on East 7th Street for years, Rudy hired others to do the cooking. When the younger Cisneros added migas and huevos rancheros to the menu, he pioneered what has become a citywide tradition: the Mexican breakfast. Soon Cisco's, as Rudy called his eatery, gained fame as a gathering place for politicians and celebrities.

Lyndon Johnson was well-known for enjoying a Bloody Mary with breakfast at his regular visits. Cisneros was loved not only for his Mexican fare but also for his humor and generosity. Daughter Ruth Ann once remembered, "My dad was a real soft touch." A close friend recalled, "Rudy probably gave away as much food as he sold." Rudy's funeral in 1995 attracted a large crowd of prominent Austin personalities. Today son Clovis Cisneros operates the still-popular restaurant.

Courtesy of Austin History Center, Austin Public Library PICA 26317

56. East 6th Street, south side between San Marcos Street and Medina Street
1930s

Fifth from the right stands Nash Moreno, owner of this East 6th Street service station. The fleet of taxis belonged to his friend Roy Velasquez. Paying $450 in 1931 for a 1928 Model A Ford, Velasquez then had to borrow an additional $5 for a taxi permit in order to begin operations as Roy's Taxi. In a competitive business Roy's Taxi carved out a niche with a reputation for dependability and willingness to accept minority riders.

Velasquez operated his taxi service out of Moreno's garage from 1936 to 1940. The metal building housing the garage was a later addition to the Buratti building to its right. That 1905 facility was initially shared by David Buratti's grocery store and the Castillo Restaurant. By 1912 the grocery store was the sole occupant. At the time of this photograph Buratti once again shared the building, this time with the Casino Bar.

East 6th Street, south side between San Marcos Street and Medina Street
2004

Roy's Taxi's trademark light green vehicles are a common sight in contemporary Austin. Roy died in 1981, but his children and relatives continue to run the family business. Nash Moreno remained in business on 6th Street long after Roy's Taxi left the premises in 1940. His 1988 obituary in the *Austin American-Statesman* listed him as a member of both the Austin Parks and Recreation Board and the Garagemen's Association. David Buratti moved a house onto a lot just down the street from his grocery store, where he lived the rest of his life. Buratti Grocery was a favorite of local residents until closing in 1963. The future of the now vacant Buratti-Moreno Building is unclear. As the historic structure nears its 100th anniversary, developers and preservationists are at odds over what to do with the site. An article in the *Austin Chronicle* asks the question, "What is a community trying to preserve through historic zoning?" In the same report one resident answers, "Without cultural landmarks, all our lives become a little poorer."

Courtesy of Center for American History, UT-Austin CN Number 11882

57. East 12th Street at Comal Street, northeast corner
1930s

Ernest Eisenbeiser opened his East End Saloon (later Eisenbeiser's Cafe) at East12th Street and Comal Street in 1910. The second story provided living space for Ernest, wife Louise, and daughters Emma and Kathryne. Ernest was born in Baden, Germany, emigrated to America in 1878, and moved to Texas in 1903. He worked with Emil Bohls in a Pflugerville meat market before opening his first cafe in Dessau in 1907. The East 12th streetcar line (see tracks in the photograph) connected with the 6th Street line at Waller Street, which in turn ran directly to Congress Avenue.

East 12th Street at Comal Street, northeast corner
2004

"Pop" Eisenbeiser ran the family business until his death in 1947. In the hands of other owners the building suffered the same gradual decline as the surrounding neighborhood. According to Pastor Tony Johnson, whose Ministry of Challenge moved onto the premises in 1996, "the very building we occupy now was a well-known nightclub, crack house, and brothel." Focusing on "healing through the Bible" the ministry provides support and temporary quarters for recovering drug addicts, alcoholics, former prisoners, and the homeless. Assistant executive director Gary Bradford attests to the resulting positive effect on the neighborhood, "You don't see people selling dope on the corner any more." Although the streetcar tracks are long-gone, the name "Eisenbeiser" remains stamped into the concrete steps along the building's front.

III. South of the River

"The bright and sparkling waters of the Colorado"

"The bright and sparkling waters of the Colorado, as they go gliding along its banks, laughing in the sunshine seem to say;
'All hail to the invention of man, I will bear you upon my bosom for his joy, and accommodation. Oh! beautiful City,
at whose base my waters have played in the days of your infancy and quietude, I will now support the wealth
of golden grain, and the products of other lands, that shall flow into thy lap. And when thou art decked
with the splendor of coming years, I will murmur low and sing the requiem of the past.'"

— *Austin Record*, November 26, 1869, reporting on completion
of the first bridge in Austin to span the Colorado River

On a June day in 1935 a raging, flooded Colorado River once again crashed through its restraining dam southwest of Austin. Wild torrents of water swept past and into the city. When the walls of the city's power plant caved in, residents found themselves fighting for life and property without the aid of electricity or, ironically, running water. Flood waters carried away homes, businesses, and a few unfortunate people. South Congress Avenue below Barton Springs Road buckled under the weight of ten feet of water, shutting off access to the concrete bridge spanning the river.

But the bridge itself held. Under the watchful eyes of Governor James Allred seated on the structure's north rail, the swollen river tried but could not swamp South Austin's vital link to downtown. Unlike the 1869 pontoon bridge which washed away a year after its construction, this sturdier span faced the river's wrath and survived. Thus, within days of what was arguably Austin's most damaging flood ever, city residents could again cross back and forth over the Colorado.

When Edwin Waller placed the Texas capital on the north bank of the Colorado River he in effect sentenced the land across the river to years of lagging development. The threat of Indian raids along the shore opposite town loomed constantly in the city's early years. Later

citizens were loathe to situate south of the river and be forced to rely on undependable ferries for transport to and from work. Failure of the pontoon bridge as well as a later wooden bridge collapsing under a herd of cattle in 1876 must have shaken confidence in development on the river's south bank. Not until the city extended a streetcar line across the Colorado River Bridge into South Austin in 1910 did many area residents begin to look across the river. Even so, the 1935 flood proved the danger of building too close to the water's edge. Construction of Tom Miller Dam on top of the two collapsed dams in 1940 seemed a step in the right direction, but it was the further construction of a series of dams farther upriver that proved decisive. Finally, after a century of uncertainty, Austin residents could build in South Austin without fear of being stranded or washed away in a rainstorm.

As the city filled in along the river it also expanded on its southern edge. Travelers from the south approached Austin along the old Post Road, later designated Highway 2 and then US Highway 81. Within city limits the highway became South Congress Avenue before crossing the river at the concrete bridge. As automobile travel increased, South Congress became lined with so-called tourist courts offering cheaper lodging than downtown hotels. Restaurants and movie theaters also

AUSTIN, TEXAS

moved into the area, in part drawn by the heavy tourist traffic.

South Austin prosperity suffered when Interstate Highway 35 began diverting travelers away from South Congress Avenue in the 1950s. By then, however, much of the area had already been developed. Thus Penn Field, built as a military air base in 1918 far south of the city, finds new life today as the Austin Design Center on South Congress Avenue in the heart of an urbanized South Austin.

Contemporary South Austin fights to retain its blue-collar identity. An area of town traditionally proud of its unpretentiousness now finds itself home to an upscale convention hotel, as well as a growing number of "clothing boutiques" and hair salons . Nevertheless, the region south of the river remains unique. In an era in which city residents encourage one another with bumper stickers and T-shirts to "Keep Austin Weird," South Austin leads the field.

58. Downtown view, looking north opposite the foot of Colorado Street
1929

Courtesy of Austin History Center, Austin Public Library C00657-B

By the 1920s periodic flooding still limited development on the south bank of the Colorado River. The lack of obstructing buildings in the foreground of this photograph renders downtown landmarks easy to spot. At right the Congress Avenue Bridge points north toward the Capitol Building projecting over the skyline. Congress Avenue is flanked on either side by the Scarbrough Building (1) and the Littlefield Building (2). The skeletal frame of the Norwood Building (3), soon to eclipse the height of the two earlier skyscrapers, reaches skyward to the left of the Capitol. To the right of the Littlefield Building is the 43-year-old Driskill Hotel (4). St. Mary's Academy (5) surveys the area from atop its hill a bit farther to the east. East of St. Mary's is St. David's Episcopal Church (6). On the horizon at far left the three towers of the University of Texas Old Main Building pierce the sky (7). The columns of the Post Office Building (8) stand out below Old Main.

Downtown view, looking north opposite the foot of Colorado Street
2004

Except for the Congress Avenue Bridge the march of progress has obstructed or obliterated all of the landmarks seen in the historic photograph. Construction of Longhorn Dam in East Austin transformed the Colorado River into the more serene Town Lake. At left, on the south shore of Town Lake, the Hyatt Regency Hotel completely blocks a view of downtown. Old Main and St. Mary's Academy have been demolished; the other buildings from the earlier photograph survive but can no longer be seen from this vantage point. Austin's newest skyscraper, the Frost Bank Tower at center with peaked roof pointing between two clouds, is merely the latest in a long line of skyscrapers to top the Norwood Building and is now the tallest building in the city.

Courtesy of Austin History Center, Austin Public Library C00621

59. South Congress Avenue, looking north between James Street and Nellie Street
1914

Only the streetcar tracks leading to the Capitol in the distance betray the urban nature of South Congress Avenue in this photograph. In 1846 James Gibson Swisher moved his family to a bluff overlooking the Colorado River and the city of Austin to the north. Within a few years Swisher achieved prosperity through a variety of astute business moves. Opening a ferry across the river in 1852 enabled Swisher to deliver travelers from the south to the foot of Congress Avenue, where he also operated a tavern and hotel. That same year Swisher granted the county right-of-way to build a road to San Antonio through his property. The San Antonio Road, also called the Post Road because of its use as a mail route, offered the first direct connection between San Antonio and the state capital. Swisher capitalized on this by establishing stagecoach service between the two

cities. In 1877 Swisher's son John subdivided 23 acres of the family farm for sale as residential property and established South Congress Avenue along the Post Road. Success eluded the younger Swisher; in 1891 there were only eight buildings along the Avenue, one of which, Leonard Eck's dry goods store, is seen in the photograph with the slightly taller facade than its adjoining neighbor. Completion of a wider, sturdier bridge across the Colorado River in 1910 encouraged the laying of streetcar tracks from the river south past the Deaf and Dumb School (immediately north of Eck's building). Guaranteed quick downtown access, residents for the first time flocked to the area. By 1912 Edd Odiorne had opened a drug store in a new building next to the old Eck store, which was now in use as a post office.

South Congress Avenue, looking north between James Street and Nellie Street
2004

South Congress Avenue remained a dirt road until 1931. Increasing tourist traffic along the highway from San Antonio in the 1920s and 1930s led to the establishment of numerous restaurants and "motor courts" along the southern entrance to the city. A period of economic decline then followed the construction of other highway routes from the south in the 1960s and 1970s. Resurgence came with the appearance of a corridor of "funky" locally-owned businesses (including Mexican folk art seller Turquoise Door). The Avenue currently seems to be undergoing another transformation to trendy "SoCo," as suggested by the hair salon and clothing boutique now occupying the buildings seen in the 1914 photograph. The trees north of these structures line the eastern extent of the grounds for The Texas State School For the Deaf, which opened in 1857 well south of the city as the State School For the Deaf and Dumb.

143

Courtesy of Austin History Center, Austin Public Library C07084

60. South Congress Avenue at Live Oak Street, northwest corner
1940

"Blaze of Light to Illuminate South Congress." So exclaimed an *Austin American* headline over a report on the "Gala Opening" of the Austin Theater August 18, 1939. Governor O'Daniel, Mayor Tom Miller, "and other notables" were among the invited guests. Forty cents gained admission to a screening of *Stanley and Livingstone* starring Spencer Tracy, with all proceeds going to "some Austin charity." University of Texas fans might have been put off by the building's maroon and white exterior (these being the colors of UT's rival Texas A&M), but once inside patrons admired the "pleasant and calm" murals of Eugene Gilbow, the beveled mirrors, and the "simple

and dignified" stairway. Aldred Campbell's cows had once grazed on the site of the new theater. F. L. Long later acquired the land and built the first house on the spot. Long's father M. M. Long had operated a stagecoach and livery stable for years on the northeast corner of Ninth Street and Congress Avenue (the building still stands). After selling the land for the theater, the younger Long moved his house to a point farther north on South Congress. At that time the Austin Theater marked the southern extent of the Avenue. Its marquee reading "Austin" was "one of the first sights to greet travelers entering the city from the south."

South Congress Avenue at Live Oak Street, northwest corner
2004

By the 1970s South Congress Avenue was well into the commercial decline instigated by the construction of Interstate Highway 35 and Mopac Expressway. The Austin Theater held on until 1977, when new owners ended its run as a new-release movie house and began showing X-rated films. According to a local police officer these new proprietors were "hooker-friendly," and soon prostitutes openly strolled the sidewalks in front of the building. Despite regular prostitution sting operations, the illicit trade flourished through years of service to its "shady clientele." In 1999 Juan Creixel of CSA Realty Group purchased the renamed Cinema West Theater. Renovation preserved the structure's form but not its function. The former "blaze of light" on South Congress Avenue is now an office building.

Courtesy of Austin History Center, Austin Public Library PICA 02206

61. Barton Springs Road, looking west at South 1st Street
1936

When Virgil and Rosa McPhail moved from Beaumont to Austin in 1924, Virgil dreamed of a career as a Baptist preacher. Initially the couple supported themselves by operating the Hokey Pokey Grocery on East 6th. In 1927 Virgil bought a small house and four acres of land on the south side of an unpaved lane known as Barton Springs Road. Rosa planted extensive flower and vegetable gardens in the rich soil. Virgil built a greenhouse and flower cottage. At first the McPhail's sold the vegetables and flowers solely in their grocery store. But by 1930 McPhail's Wayside Gardens stood alone as an independent business. During the Depression Austinites paid $1 for the chance to take as many flowers as could be carried away. As can be seen in this 1936 photograph, the McPhail daughters, Rosa Nell, Ruthie, and Janette, enjoyed much open space in which to play and ride the family's horse.

Barton Springs Road, looking west at South 1st Street
2004

Virgil and Rosa divorced in the mid 1930s. Rosa remained in the cottage on Barton Springs Road until her death in 1978. She ran the business by herself until the late 1960s, when she passed it on to daughter Janette. Amanda Van Orden, who started work at Wayside after dropping out of school at age 14 in 1946, bought the shop in the 1970s. It is now owned by Gerald Ledbetter. McPhail's Florist is the oldest structure on modern Barton Springs Road. The building is just visible to the left of the towering pecan tree under which the McPhail daughters once played. Younger Austin icon Sandy's is also seen at left. Palmer Auditorium occupies the land across the street.

Courtesy of Austin History Center, Austin Public Library PICA 17617

62. South 1st Street, looking north at Barton Springs Road
1939

In 1939 much of the state capital south of the Colorado River consisted of open fields, dusty streets, wooded lots, and places like The Steer. Only Congress Avenue crossed the river, while future thoroughfares such as South 1st Street dead-ended at the south bank. Walter Johnson's advertisement for horse-shoeing and repairing shows that city blacksmiths had not quite faded away. Downtown Austin lies straight ahead, little more than a stone's throw from this rural scene.

South 1st Street, looking north at Barton Springs Road
2004

No more dust and plenty of pavement! Nothing remains to disguise the urban location of this intersection. A six-lane bridge guides traffic across Town Lake toward a modern landscape of steel and glass towers. The previously empty field at left is occupied by Palmer Auditorium, soon to undergo a major transformation into a performing arts center. On the far side of the bridge the new city hall under construction is already drawing praise for the innovative look it contributes to the skyline.

St. Elmo-Tel -- Austin's finest Motel
One Mile South of the Capital City -- U. S. 81

63. South Congress Avenue at St. Elmo Road, northeast corner
c. 1940

Who could have resisted the following polite advertisement in the May 12, 1940 *Austin Daily Tribune*? "We cordially invite you to come out this afternoon 3 to 7 o'clock and inspect St. Elmo-tel, the finest motel in Texas." "Strategically located" one mile from the city limits on Highway 81 South, the facility contained "nineteen units now ready for the traveling public." An accompanying article boasted of the usual array of modern conveniences, including "hot water instantly available at the turn of the faucet." Each unit contained a kitchen equipped with refrigerator, gas stove, cabinet, and sink "combined into one compact unit occupying only eight square feet of floor space." Golfers could enjoy the practice tees while "less energetic guests" could amuse themselves on the croquet court. The motel was named for the historic St. Elmo community, whose post office once sat across the highway.

South Congress Avenue at St. Elmo Road, northeast corner
2004

St. Elmo-tel, now usually referred to as the St. Elmo Motel, lives on. Offering 22 rooms, still with kitchens but now also with cable TV and premium movie channels, the St. Elmo provides inexpensive lodging for short- and long-term stays. A 1970 brochure promoting the motel bragged of "Central Texas the Tourist's Paradise." From the St. Elmo one could visit the University of Texas with its "well equipped libraries" or cruise along one of the "beautiful, well-planned scenic drives . . . to the finest series of dams and lakes in the south." These days the hyperbole has diminished. A visitor would more likely be attracted to the St. Elmo by its cheap rates than its convenience, comfort, or beauty. Nevertheless, the motel has endured while many others along South Congress Avenue have not.

Hotel Elegance and Comfort
Face Brick Exterior . . .
Carpeted Apartments . . . Private Dressing Room . . . Elegant Tiled Bath . . . Solid Maple Furniture . . . Beautyrest Mattresses . . . Venetian Blinds . . . Private Telephone.

San José Court

1310-1320 South Congress Avenue
U. S. Highway 81 - - State 2 and 29

Austin, Texas

Tourist Court Conveniences
Wide Court, artistically landscaped . . . Large Casement Windows . . . Private Garage attached to each Apartment, with overhead door and Cylinder Lock.

**64. South Congress Avenue, west side between Gibson Street and James Street
post-1936**

Nineteenth century travelers from the south entered Austin by way of the Post Road (also called the San Antonio Road), which in turn connected with Congress Avenue. In 1917 the newly formed Texas State Highway Department named this thoroughfare Highway 2. By the time of its re-designation in 1936 as U. S. Highway 81, numerous "tourist courts" lined both sides of the street. The "ultramodern" San Jose Court, which opened in1936, was typical with its one-story line of bungalows surrounding a central courtyard. Guests relaxed in the "Hotel Elegance and Comfort" provided by the "Carpeted Apartments" with "Elegant Tiled Bath" and "Beauty-rest Mattresses." A guest's automobile was safe in its own individual garage equipped "with overhead door and Cylinder Lock."

South Congress Avenue, west side between Gibson Street and James Street
2004

Business boomed for the tourist courts until the 1960s, when newly created Mopac Expressway and Interstate Highway 35 began siphoning off much of the traffic coming into the city from the south. Back then a brothel favored by Texas legislators supposedly operated out of the San Jose Court. When the Senate lacked a quorum, one could ring a buzzer at the front desk of the motel via a direct line from the Capitol. San Jose briefly saw service as a church Bible school in the 1970s, before falling from grace again as a "haven for drug users, pimps, and prostitutes." Local lawyer Liz Lambert purchased the property in 1995 and restored the run-down landmark. The renamed San Jose Hotel is once again a popular destination for respectable travelers.

Courtesy of Austin History Center, Austin Public Library C07469

**65. Dawson Road, looking east between Riverside Drive and Barton Springs Road
1956**

Manager Connie Ryan (#8) watches his Austin Senators take batting practice at Disch Field in April 1956. Former major-leaguers Mike Clark (#11) and Ted Wilks (#24) await their turn at bat. "Austin's grand old man of baseball" Ed Knebel enlisted Dupre Johnson and the Austin Jaycees in a successful drive to convince the City Council to appropriate funds for building a new baseball stadium. When the city matched the $16,000 raised by the Jaycees, architects began in November 1941 to develop plans for the new park. But Pearl Harbor intervened to divert attention and funding away from the project. Disch Field finally opened for Knebel's Austin Pioneers in 1947. After nine mediocre seasons Knebel sold the team, paving the way for Allen Russell to move his Class AA Beaumont team of the Texas League to Austin in time for the 1956 season. The moniker Senators prevailed over several others under consideration, including Jets, Braves, and Capitals.

Dawson Road, looking east between Riverside Drive and Barton Springs Road
2004

Over its relatively short life Disch Field witnessed the play of many future major league stars. Hall-of-Famer Phil Niekro pitched for the home team, while other local heroes included Ralph Garr, Cito Gaston, and Dusty Baker. The Milwaukee Braves acquired the lease on Disch Field in 1965 and changed the name of the Austin team to match its own. By then the stadium badly needed an array of expensive repairs and updates, but the team lacked adequate funds. The deteriorating condition of the stadium coupled with lackluster team performance hurt attendance enough to cause the parent club to cut its Austin ties after the 1967 season. In a 1968 article headlined "Death at Disch Field," the *Austin Statesman* mourned the already decrepit appearance of the ballpark: "You want to cry a bucket of tears? Go see Disch Field." A year later the facility was demolished. With careful inspection today one can still see the grassy, graded elevation that was once the playground of Austin's baseball heroes.

Courtesy of Austin History Center, Austin Public Library C00077-A

66. Barton Springs, looking southeast
c. 1886

In 1860 native Pennsylvanian John Rabb had earned a long, peaceful retirement when at age 63 he purchased land along the banks of Barton Creek. A younger Rabb had arrived in Texas in 1822 as one of Stephen F. Austin's "Old Three Hundred" original colonists. He earned a bonus of three leagues of land from the Mexican government for building the first grist mill in Texas in what is now Fayette County. His gratitude evidently having faded, Rabb battled the Mexicans as part of Sam Houston's army at San Jacinto. After independence he fought with the Republic in its efforts to

evict or destroy the region's Indian residents. John Rabb died in 1861, only a year after moving to his new home south of the state's capital. Youngest son Gail, the only child of John to accompany him to the Austin area, built the city's first ice factory within his grist mill on Barton Creek in 1871. Farther up the creek he built another mill, which burned in 1886. Undeterred, Rabb rebuilt on the foundation of the destroyed mill just below the dam of cedar logs pictured at right. All of these mills exploited the constant, heavy flow of water coming from several underground springs along Barton Creek.

Barton Springs, looking southeast
2004

A. J. Zilker in 1907 bought much of Gail Rabb's Barton Creek homestead, including the now-famous springs. By 1913 Rabb's mill lay in ruins and was torn down by the city of Austin. Four years later Zilker donated 35 acres along the creek (with the springs) to Austin Public Schools on condition that the city would then buy the land from the school system for $100,000. For $200,000 in 1932 Austin gained title to the remaining 330 acres around the springs through another three-way deal involving Zilker, the school system, and the city. Construction in 1923 of the concrete dam visible at far left created the spring-fed pool still in use. A flood-control tunnel diverting the creek around the pool was added in 1974. Runoff from area development intermittently pollutes the pool and forces its temporary closure, a controversy which has dominated local politics since the 1980s. The issue reached the statehouse when local developer Gary Bradley found legislative support for weakening the local ordinance protecting Barton Creek. Throughout such political maneuvering Barton Springs has continued its supply of cold, fresh water to the pool known by city residents as The Jewel of Austin.

IV. West Austin

Toward the "Violet Crown"

"The drawing-rooms of one of the most magnificent private residences in Austin are a blaze of lights. Carriages line the streets in front, and from gate to doorway is spread a velvet carpet, on which the delicate feet of the guests may tread. The occasion is the entree into society of one of the fairest buds in the City of the Violet Crown."
— from *Tictocq, the Great French Detective, in Austin* by O. Henry, 1894

Picture West Austin's past and visualize as wide a range of experiences as exists in this city. Jacob Harrell could have wandered from his cabin in Waterloo over to Shoal Creek in 1838 and encountered Indians ambling along an ancient trail following the creek bed. A few years later local residents walked this trail in fear of meeting one of the dangerous outlaws said to be hiding along the steep banks. A visitor to the area in the 1850s would have seen African-American slaves toiling on a vast plantation ruled from an elegant mansion on the west side of the creek. A decade later that visitor would have seen many of those same people at work building a poor, but free community called Clarksville in a small corner of the mansion's grounds. In the early twentieth century a grandson of the mansion's former owner subdivided most of the one-time plantation and created a neighborhood still known for its grandeur and wealth. At the same time residents of Clarksville lit their homes with kerosene lamps and walked unpaved streets lined by open sewers.

In Austin's early days a ride out past West Avenue was viewed as a trip to the country. Augustus Koch's 1887 bird's eye view map of the city shows very few structures beyond Shoal Creek. Most that were present lay strung along the tracks of the International and Great Northern Railroad which roughly followed West 3rd Street out of town. Not long after a train cut through Clarksville heading north it was riding in open country.

When Austin's first dam was completed in 1895, city residents were quick to take advantage of the streetcar line built to carry riders out to the new Lake McDonald. Suddenly the city's western edge seemed closer. A day in the country then meant passing *through* West Austin on West 6th Street before it turned into Dam Boulevard and terminated at the lake. Pleasure seekers could spend the day swimming, fishing, picnicking, and riding the steamboat *Ben Hur* before returning by the same route as night fell.

Rural West Austin's end became inevitable with subdivision of the Pease plantation after World War I. Developers built Enfield Road as an extension of 15th Street leading into the newly created neighborhoods. Increasing use of automobiles offered quick access to homesites which otherwise would have had little appeal. Clarksville, the small community which had *intentionally* been established far out of town, suddenly occupied desirable real estate and was forced into a decades-long fight for survival.

West Austin's variety extends as well to individual landmarks. The demolished Confederate Veteran's Home once sat on grounds along West 6th Street not too far from the I&GN tracks. Still overlooking Shoal Creek and thus Austin itself is "The Castle", former home of the

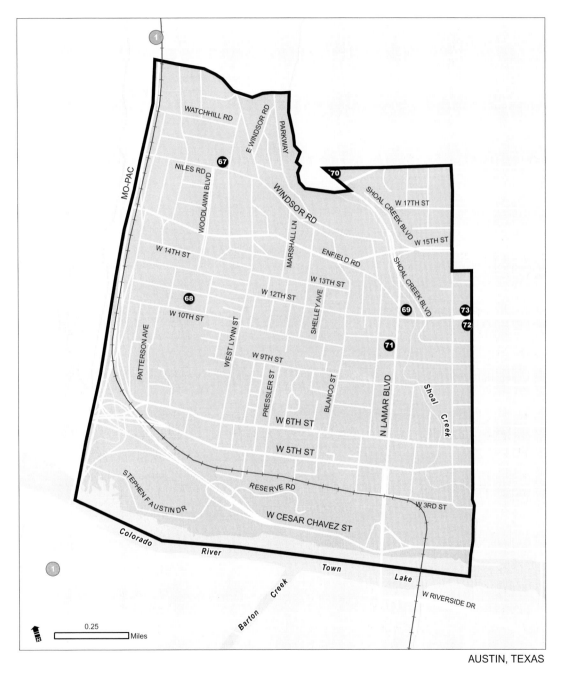

Texas Military Institute. Centuries-old Treaty Oak on Baylor Street survived an intentional poisoning in 1989 to remain a popular tourist attraction. Tonkawa Indians had long used the tree as a meeting place before supposedly signing a peace treaty with Stephen F. Austin under its canopy.

The modern West Austin resident might live in a 19th-century bungalow or a 21st-century highrise. She might dine on roast duck at the most elegant restaurant in town or munch on a slab of barbecue at an outside table under a sign reading, "Need no teef to eat my beef." She might steer her Lexus into the landscaped driveway fronting a $2 million home or wait for her train at the Amtrak station behind an old iron foundry. In short, if there has been *one* common theme characterizing West Austin over the years it is that there has been *no* common theme characterizing West Austin over the years.

AUSTIN, TEXAS

Courtesy of Austin History Center, Austin Public Library PICH 02200

67. Woodlawn, 6 Niles Road, looking north
c. 1884

After Texas Comptroller James Shaw purchased 650 acres of land west of Austin in separate deals with Mirabeau Lamar and Joseph Moreland, he commissioned Abner Cook to build a new home on the property. In 1854 Cook completed the largest and most expensive house of his career, the magnificent Greek Revival mansion shown in this photograph. Shaw brought his new bride to Austin in 1857, but the following year the couple left for New Orleans because of Mrs. Shaw's declining health. Shaw rented the house to Judge R. J. Towns and left the grounds in the care of two of his slaves, married couple Billy and Jane. At about the same time Governor Elisha Pease and his wife Lucadia were looking for a permanent Austin home. Learning of this, Shaw, by now living in Baltimore, offered the house to Pease for $15,000, or $5,000 less than he had paid to have it built. Fully aware of the reasons for Shaw's desire to sell, Pease drove a hard bargain. In July 1859 he acquired the house and 186 acres for $14,000. The name Woodlawn originated with the mansion's new residents. Governor Pease died in 1883, a year after the death of daughter Carrie Augusta Pease Graham. Carrie's death left the three children in this photograph to be raised by her mother Lucadia and her sister Julia. Here Grandma Pease (seated on porch) supervises her grandchildren on the south lawn of the house. Carrie Margaret and her brother Richard Niles sit under a tree near their grandmother while Marshall rides his pony at right.

Woodlawn, 6 Niles Road, looking north
2004

Woodlawn remained in the Pease family for 98 years. At its height the plantation encompassed all of the land bounded by present-day West 12th Street (south), Shoal Creek (east), West 24th Street (north), and Exposition Boulevard (west). Richard Niles Graham married a granddaughter of Walter Tips in 1910 and brought her to Woodlawn to live. In 1916 Niles donated four acres adjoining Shoal Creek to the city. This was added to the 22 acres given by his grandfather years earlier to form Pease Park. Niles then subdivided the Pease estate, creating the Enfield, Westenfield, Westfield, and Tarrytown neighborhoods. The name Enfield came from the Connecticut hometown of Governor Elisha Pease. Many of the streets in the neighborhood bear names borrowed form Connecticut. Retiring Texas Governor Allan Shivers bought the Pease mansion in December 1956, ending the lengthy tenure of the Pease family. Shivers died in 1985 but his widow Marialice stayed on at Woodlawn until her passing in 1996. The couple left the house to the University of Texas, which in turn sold it to the state. Lieutenant Governor Bob Bullock urged use of the mansion as a home for the state's governor or for visiting dignitaries. Nothing came of these plans, however, and after Bullock's death in 1999, the state put the house up for sale. Three years later local investor Jeff Sandefer purchased the property for over $3 million.

Courtesy of Austin History Center, Austin Public Library PICA 24451

68. West 11th Street, south side between Toyath Street and Charlotte Street
post-1935

Charles Griffin sought a fresh start following his emancipation at the close of the Civil War. He changed his surname to Clark, bought two acres of land from ex-Confederate general Nathan Shelley, and, by subdividing the property, created the township of Clarksville. The land at one time was part of Governor Elisha Pease's enormous antebellum plantation west of town. Knowing that they were unwelcome to live within Austin's city limits, many former slaves were happy to build a home in Clarksville. Their jobs in the city center lay not too far away, yet the distance from town provided relative safety from harassment by whites. In 1871 the Reverend Jacob Fontaine gathered with other Clarksville community leaders in the home of Mary Smith and established the Second Baptist Church, later renamed Sweet Home Missionary Baptist Church. Fontaine presided over services in the Smith home until the congregation purchased the site in this photograph for $50 in 1882. The structure pictured here was erected in 1935 and is the fourth church building on the premises. From its inception Sweet Home played a central role in binding the community of Clarksville together.

West 11th Street, south side between Toyath Street and Charlotte Street
2004

Sweet Home Missionary Baptist Church and the community of Clarksville have survived against almost impossible odds. By the early 20th century the City of Austin, originally indifferent to the township, was displaying increasing hostility as a result of pressure from white developers who coveted the area and its surroundings. Pease Estate heir R. Niles Graham began developing the former plantation in the 1920s as the Enfield Addition. Austin extended city services to the new, wealthier neighborhood but not to Clarksville. The city's 1928 master plan advised "that all the facilities and conveniences be provided the Negroes in this district (east Austin), as an incentive to draw the Negro population to this area." For the next several decades Clarksville residents stubbornly held on despite unpaved roads, lack of water and electricity, little official educational support, and periodic floods. Although city government abandoned its official antagonistic policy in 1954, street paving did not begin until 1975. Clarksville suffered a major defeat in 1968 when city council approved construction of the Mopac Expressway. The new highway replaced the community's western third. In 1975 the area averted what would have been a death blow when it successfully opposed plans to build a highway connecting Mopac with Interstate Highway 35 to the east. Throughout these and other battles Sweet Home Missionary Baptist Church has provided focus to the community's quest for survival.

Courtesy of Austin History Center, Austin Public Library C05508

69. Ruiz Street at West 12th Street, northeast corner
post-1916

"Don't you think groceries from a store like this will just naturally taste better than if bought in some ugly run down looking place? Of course they will! At the Main Entrance to Enfield One of Austin's Picturesque Additions." So exclaimed an early advertisement for Enfield Grocery, built in 1916 at West 12th Street and Ruiz Street. Niles Graham carved Enfield out of his grandfather Elisha Pease's antebellum plantation, thereby enticing affluent Austinites out of the downtown area. He erected the German-style building in the photograph as a pub, only to be frustrated by enactment of Prohibition. Emil Kuehne then opened a grocery with "the best lines of staple and fancy groceries and country produce" available by delivery "not only in Enfield but all over town." The ornate decorative eaves on the building were created by famed local woodcarver Peter Mansbendel.

Lamar Boulevard at West 12th Street, northeast corner
2004

With a bit of luck the modern visitor to Niles Graham's pub might encounter the ghost of Emily, former employee during the building's early illicit days. Legend tells of a second-floor brothel and speakeasy in which Emily's duties extended beyond waiting tables. In 1929 Enfield Grocery moved next door in favor of a steakhouse. Prohibition's repeal in 1933 paved the way for The Tavern, still quenching Austin's thirst 71 years later. The city sought unsuccessfully to raze The Tavern in the 1940s when it widened Ruiz Street and renamed it Lamar Boulevard. Demolition threatened again in 2002 when The Tavern was forced to close because of lack of funding necessary to bring the building up to code. Steve Harren, Stan Miller, and Bob Cole then stepped in with the money for renovation, and one of Austin's favorite gathering places reopened in 2003.

Courtesy of Austin History Center, Austin Public Library PICA 20378

70. Lamar Boulevard, looking south at West 19th Street
pre-1940

Lamar Boulevard was once a dirt road coursing along Shoal Creek across from the old Pease plantation. Former Texas governor and slave-holder Elisha Marshall Pease occupied the 365-acre country estate after purchasing it from Texas Comptroller James Shaw in 1859. In this view, downtown Austin lies out of sight in the center distance while Shoal Creek is to the viewer's right. Union soldiers camped in this area during Reconstruction. Many succumbed to an 1866 epidemic and were buried along the banks of the creek. Marshall Pease donated a 23-acre strip of land along Shoal Creek to the city in 1875 for use as a public park.

Lamar Boulevard, looking south at Martin Luther King Jr. Boulevard
2004

After being paved in the 1940s, Lamar Boulevard became a major north-south route through the city. Before construction of Interstate Highway 35 the thoroughfare became the Dallas Highway as it headed north out of town. Most of the park donated by and named for Marshall Pease lies sandwiched between Shoal Creek and the modern road between 15th and 24th streets. Looking southeast from the park provides a magnificent view of downtown Austin. The tallest skyscraper in this view and in the city is the Frost Bank Tower. Opening in 2004, the building is visible from almost any distant vantage point just as the Capitol Building once was.

Courtesy of Austin History Center, Austin Public Library PICH 04060

71. 1111 West Mesquite Street, looking northwest
1876

In this photograph young cadets line up in front of the turreted Texas Military Institute. Established in Bastrop in the 1850s, the private academy relocated to Austin in 1870 when its Bastrop facilities proved inadequate. After luring the Institute with a building fund composed of $10,000 worth of gold bullion, the City of Austin purchased a 32-acre tract on a bluff overlooking Shoal Creek. The Institute then constructed the castle-like structure on the property in June 1870. Mindful of its location in the recently defeated and still occupied south, TMI stressed its goal of "governing the Cadets and giving them regular and healthful physical exercise—*not to train officers for the profession of arms.*" Cadets observed strict rules or risked immediate expulsion. According to a school catalog, "Dismissal is instant if a cadet plays cards, bets on games of skill, or visits the bar rooms or disreputable resorts of the city." "Manly sports and exercises," however, were "properly encouraged." The administrator felt it necessary to state, "This institute is in no sense an asylum for vicious, depraved or unmanageable boys . . . ." Although the school claimed to be "free from all sectarian influences," attendance of *some* type of religious service was mandatory. ". . . the Cadets march to the different city churches, in rotation. Communicants are allowed to attend their respective churches out of ranks."

1111 West 11th Street, looking northwest
2004

During its ten years of existence, the Texas Military Institute housed an annual average of 99 cadets in barracks capable of holding 400. When in 1879 the state organized Texas Agricultural and Mechanical College (now Texas A&M University), TMI president John Garland James and the entire faculty left Austin for positions at the new state military institution. The private military academy closed its doors. From 1884 to 1887 Jacob Bickler's academy occupied the old military castle. When Bickler left, the south half of the building was removed, leaving only the single tower pictured here. After decades as a private residence, the building was purchased for office space by controversial real estate developer Gary Bradley in 2001.

Courtesy of Austin History Center, Austin Public Library PICA 07111

72. Rio Grande Street, west side between West 11th Street and West 12th Street
post-1876

Edwin Waller's 1839 city plan of Austin called for a university on the block bounded by Rio Grande Street, West Avenue, Mulberry (11th) Street, and College Avenue (12th Street). In 1876 the Austin School Board established the Austin Graded School in the new building in this photograph. This was the first school in Texas erected with public funds. Classrooms operated under strict rules of conduct, including "Students may not communicate with each other in any way." Later the school became known as Pease School for Governor Elisha Marshall Pease. Austin High School enrolled its first students here in 1881 and temporarily used the third floor for its classes. After the city built John T. Allan Junior High School on the block to the north, Pease School operated solely as a facility for elementary education.

Rio Grande Street, west side between West 11th Street and West 12th Street
2004

Pease School today is the oldest continuously operating public school in Texas. The edifice has endured an 1892 fire, building additions in 1916 and 1926, and an extensive remodeling in 1949. The school's website boasts of it as Austin Independent School District's "best kept little secret." Touted advantages include small classes, a diverse student body, "veteran" teachers, and the fact that "Pease students, even kindergartners, know most of the teachers and staff as well as other Pease students and parents."

Courtesy of Austin History Center, Austin Public Library C00802

73. Rio Grande Street at West 12th Street, northwest corner
1930s

In 1881 a group of 48 Austin teenagers climbed to the top floor of the Pease School building to begin classes in the city's first high school. Over the next 19 years students followed the school as it migrated through three other facilities, including First Baptist Church, the temporary state Capitol, and Smith Opera House. When the district erected a permanent high school building at Trinity Street and East 9th Street, Austin High's nomadic days seemed to be over. But in 1925 overcrowding forced yet another move into the building in this photograph. Built in 1916 as John T. Allan Junior High School, this structure lies immediately north of Pease School located on the block reserved by Edwin Waller in 1839 for an educational facility. The high school and junior high school merely swapped places in 1925 with the junior high moving across town to the high school's former home. Students must have enjoyed the convenience of the streetcar line running in front of Austin High School. But as is evident in the photograph, many also lived close enough to reach class on foot.

Rio Grande Street at West 12th Street, northwest corner
2004

Austin High School changed its name in 1953 to Stephen F. Austin High School to reflect the fact that it was no longer the city's only institute of secondary education for white students (Anderson High School in East Austin had been educating minority children since 1889). Even so, by the 1970s the building was too small for its purpose. In 1975 Austin High abandoned its Rio Grande campus for a much larger complex built on the north shore of Town Lake, using land once owned by Andrew Zilker. The old building then took another step up the educational ladder when it was acquired by Austin Community College. The marker at the base of the moonlight tower attests to the historic value of the structure. Few students reach class on foot any more, while those who employ public transportation rely on the city buses which stop at the shelter at center right.

V. HYDE PARK
Austin's first suburb

"I had $850 when I came to Austin. This I spent in securing my [streetcar] franchise, to enable me to build a road
to the tract of land I had secured north of the city and which I proposed to open up."

— HYDE PARK DEVELOPER MONROE SHIPE

If Mirabeau Lamar in 1838 had turned his back to the Colorado River and gazed north from the rise on which the Capitol now sits, he would have seen a dense forest of centuries-old oak trees covering an area rich in game. For generations Tonkawa, Lipan Apache, and Comanche Indians had occupied and hunted this land. That life ended when Austin's early inhabitants destroyed the forest and used the trees to construct their new town.

Once the trees and Indians were gone, the large, smooth area which remained seemed ideal for racing horses. Following the Civil War the Capital Jockey Club Racecourse began drawing large crowds of spectators. This in turn enticed state fair organizers to purchase the land in 1872. The entire city turned out to the 80-acre site for the fair's opening November 10, 1875. Enclosed by an 8-foot fence, the fairgrounds included an exhibition hall, judges' stand, and 3,500-seat grandstand. In the fair's early years, attractions included cockfighting, a rifle gallery, and a trapshooting booth in which customers fired at live pigeons.

Despite the encouraging attendance this event in Austin never achieved consistent financial success. Heavy rain turned the 1883 fair into a muddy disaster, and after another year in central Texas the fair abandoned the state capital for Dallas. That final year in Austin was so poorly funded that the winner for the best bale of cotton had to go home without his $10 prize.

Over the next few years the abandoned fairgrounds continued to host local entertainment. Horse racing, calf roping, and even University of Texas football games lured city residents to the site. The Texas Volunteer Guard held an annual encampment which attracted companies from across the state.

Investors from Kansas City bought the old fairgrounds in 1890. When Monroe Shipe purchased the property in 1891, he initially intended to build a rail yard to serve the MKT rail line anticipated to arrive shortly. But Shipe grew impatient and changed his plans when rail construction lagged. His new idea included building a residential community called Hyde Park in this outlying area which would be connected to the city by a street rail line that he would also build.

Shipe's task was enormous, but he successfully surmounted every challenge. Battling opposition from other streetcar operators, he had his own line in service by February 1891. He convinced the city to erect its first moonlight tower in Hyde Park. He installed water mains in the area as well as gas lines, electricity, and fire hydrants. He paid for construction of the Speedway as a connecting road between Hyde Park and downtown. Shipe even planted trees along the roads built in his new neighborhood.

The plan worked. Attracted by inexpensive land and the prospect of living in a healthful, wholesome neighborhood, people flocked to purchase Shipe's lots. But not all were welcome. Early advertisements

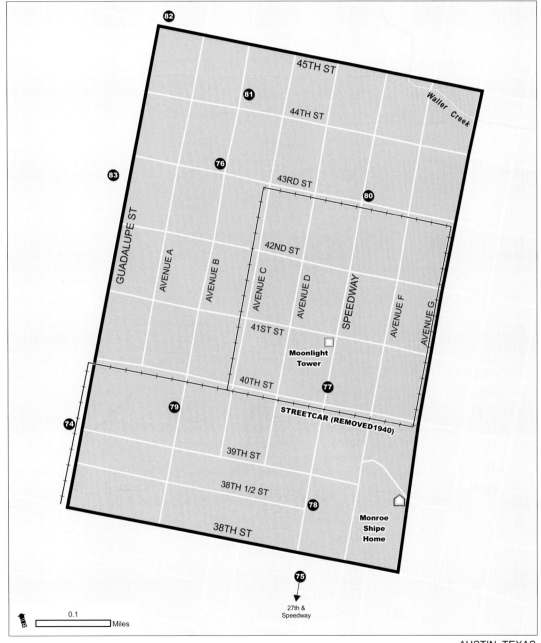

45TH ST

44TH ST

43RD ST

42ND ST

41ST ST

Moonlight
Tower

40TH ST

STREETCAR (REMOVED1940)

39TH ST

38TH 1/2 ST

38TH ST

Monroe
Shipe
Home

GUADALUPE ST

AVENUE A

AVENUE B

AVENUE C

AVENUE D

SPEEDWAY

AVENUE F

AVENUE G

Waller Creek

0.1 Miles

27th &
Speedway

AUSTIN, TEXAS

for Hyde Park clearly stated that land would be sold only to whites.

In Hyde Park's early decades, the neighborhood conveyed the feel of a town separate from Austin. Shipe originally numbered the east-west streets 1st Street through 8th Street, street names already in use in downtown Austin. As the area added churches, schools, and grocery stores, residents found less occasion to travel into town. The open, undeveloped nature of the landscape between Hyde Park and the city limits heightened the sensation of traveling between two separate communities.

As Austin engulfed and surrounded Hyde Park, neighborhood identity remained strong. Even today residents display strong commitment to maintaining the unique flavor of their area of town. Recent battles with city government over the local fire station and with Hyde Park Baptist Church regarding church expansion have illustrated that Hyde Park residents understand and appreciate the historic value of Austin's first planned suburban community.

Courtesy of Austin History Center, Austin Public Library PICA 02628

74. 39th Street, looking east at Guadalupe Street
c. 1900

Monroe Shipe arrived in Austin from Abilene, Kansas, in 1889 planning to build a railyard north of the city for the coming MKT Railroad. But slow progress on the new line sparked Shipe to embark upon a daring venture, the development of Austin's first planned suburb, Hyde Park. Realizing he would have to entice people to live far outside the business district, Shipe first laid streetcar tracks between downtown and his new community and inaugurated street rail service February 26, 1891. A nickel bought a one-way trip. If one preferred a carriage ride, "the finest drive in Texas," also known as "the Speedway," was available. Hyde Park promised "the most beautiful, healthful, and practical place for homes in the city of Austin." Attractions included free mail delivery twice a day, no limestone dust, smooth mudless roads, and the promise that "Hyde Park is exclusively for white people." Initial investors received one free lot with every two purchased. Shipe himself built one of the first homes at the corner of 39th and Avenue G, where he lived until his death in 1924.

39th Street, looking east at Guadalupe Street
2004

Despite the current appearance of its one-time picturesque entry, Hyde Park has retained its neighborhood identity. But not without a struggle. Following World War II large numbers of residents left Hyde Park for newer suburbs, and many of their former homes became run-down rental properties. University of Texas expansion in the 1960s and 1970s led to a boom in apartment complex construction in Austin. Numerous original Hyde Park houses were destroyed. Subsequently, the Hyde Park Neighborhood Association organized in an effort to preserve the residential character of the area. In 1990 the U. S. Department of the Interior added Hyde Park to the National Register for Historic Places. Today much of the original charm of the neighborhood has returned. Notable in this photograph is the Baker School at left behind Rooster Andrews Sporting Goods. This building was erected on the site of Hyde Park Pavilion, a community center which stood on the shore of now-drained Gem Lake.

Courtesy of Austin History Center, Austin Public Library PICA 02616

75. Speedway, looking south at 27th Street
1905

A century ago "the Speedway" provided direct access to downtown Austin from Hyde Park. Neighborhood developer Monroe Shipe recognized the importance of maintaining and improving such a roadway as a means of persuading city residents to buy homes so far out of town. When projected cost rose above what Shipe's MK&T Land Company could afford, he turned to the city for help. Denied municipal funds, Shipe appealed to the public in 1900. "Don't you feel an interest in having at least one good street in Austin? You use it and you should help." The *Austin Statesman* in 1905 opined ". . . to go to Hyde Park necessitates driving over this very rocky steep hill, which is almost impossible . . . it (Speedway) is the most needed and traveled by all classes of any street in the city." The rural countryside in this photograph emphasizes how distant the Hyde Park suburb seemed to Austinites of the era. Only the state university's Old Main building at right reminds the viewer that Speedway is indeed a *city* street.

Speedway, looking south at 27th Street
2004

City government allotted $8,660 in 1912 for improvements to Speedway and the cross streets of Hyde Park. Private contributions brought in another $2,600. Workers conquered the "rocky steep hill," improved street drainage, and placed ditches along the roadway to carry runoff during rainstorms. Shipe attempted to minimize dust by sprinkling streets with water. A later experiment involving sprayed oil proved too messy. The modern, paved Speedway no longer serves as a primary thoroughfare between downtown and points north. Because the University of Texas campus envelopes a several-block section of the street, through traffic is diverted east to Red River Street and west to Guadalupe Street. Today campus buildings rise along both sides of Speedway. At left is Robert Lee Moore Hall. The Sarah M. and Charles E. Seay Building (distant right) and the Speedway Garage (near right) obscure sight of the UT Tower, which replaced Old Main in the 1930s.

Courtesy of Austin History Center, Austin Public Library PICA 02623

76. 43rd Street, looking west at Avenue B
c. 1900

How isolated early Hyde Park residents must have felt! Except for the streetcar and the State Lunatic Asylum in the distance, 43rd Street (6th Street in Monroe Shipe's original plan) appears as a lonely country lane. In fact, this was not far from the truth. Most of the original Hyde Park families kept livestock, usually just a few chickens and a cow or goat. Cows could graze in empty lots, alleys, or drainage ditches, but as Hyde Park filled up some landowners began charging a small fee for this privilege. Horses remained a common sight into the 20th century. Many families maintained large gardens on empty lots purchased specifically for that purpose. Smokehouses were not uncommon, and nearby Shoal Creek offered several excellent fishing holes. Some residents hunted small game in the area such as raccoon, squirrel, or opossum. Others rode the streetcar to its terminus in rural South Austin to go after larger animals. In an age without refrigeration, rural activities such as these were less recreation than necessity.

43rd Street, looking west at Avenue B
2004

The chickens left last. Even when refrigeration enabled stores to sell eggs, some old-timers kept a few birds around just because they liked the rural sound effects. Cows, hogs, and goats disappeared soon after people began buying their meat and milk in grocery stores. Automobiles, of course, eventually supplanted horse-drawn conveyances. Large sustenance gardening became impossible as available empty lots were converted to homesites. As a *central* Austin neighborhood, today's Hyde Park no longer offers nearby hunting or fishing opportunities. Monroe Shipe's original streetcars vanished along with Austin's street rail service in 1940. Without the trees, the Austin State Hospital (the old Lunatic Asylum) would still be visible across Guadalupe Street.

Courtesy of Austin History Center, Austin Public Library C02718

77. Speedway, looking north between 40th Street and 41st Street
1897

Little need can be seen for the nocturnal lighting capability provided by this moonlight tower on the southwest corner of 41st Street and Speedway. With an eye toward the future, Hyde Park developer Monroe Shipe had two years previously convinced Austin to install the first of its 31 new towers in his proposed neighborhood. Early resident fears of deleterious effects on livestock and vegetable gardens from prolonged light exposure proved groundless. Note the rows of trees planted along Speedway. Shipe paid for such tree planting throughout Hyde Park as part of his over-all effort to lure Austinites away from the convenience of downtown living.

Speedway, looking north between 40th Street and 41st Street
2004

After 109 years Hyde Park's moonlight tower still casts its nightly glow. Early 20th century houses on either side of the block are obscured by rows of decades-old trees. Despite the disappearance of horse-drawn carriages on dusty neighborhood roads, Hyde Park retains its charm as a small, tight-knit community. There is at least one difference, however: many of today's residents are attracted by the neighborhood's *central* location in an ever-expanding city.

Courtesy of Austin History Center, Austin Public Library PICA 02625

78. Speedway, looking north between 38th Street and 39th Street
c. 1900

At first, Hyde Park was little more than a grid of dusty roads at the end of Monroe Shipe's streetcar line. Initially courting wealthier buyers, Shipe was able to sell many of the corner lots in his neighborhood for construction of large Victorian homes. When lot sales subsequently lagged and Shipe began marketing more to working class families, new construction tended toward more modest dwellings. In this photograph note the many available home sites near the intersection of Speedway and 39th Street.

Speedway, looking north between 38th Street and 39th Street
2004

Within a year of its founding in 1894, Hyde Park Baptist Church built its first permanent sanctuary on the southwest corner of 39th Street and Speedway. The congregation moved into a larger facility on the intersection's northeast corner in 1911. By the late 1940s this building proved too small, and bond sales financed construction of a third sanctuary. Known at the time as "Tatum's Folly," in recognition of pastor Scott Tatum's support for the massive structure, the new building seated 1,000 worshipers at its opening, and 1,350 after a 1967 remodeling. In 1983 Dr. Ralph Smith preached the first sermon in the church's fourth (and current) sanctuary to an overflow crowd of 2,200 faithful. The building's basement contains a television and radio studio large enough for an additional 1,000 people. Since its inception, Hyde Park Baptist Church has grown from 14 members and one small wooden building to a sprawling complex covering several blocks of the neighborhood. Many Hyde Park residents have objected to the changes inherent to such expansion. The latest conflict centers upon a proposed five-story parking garage desired by the church.

Courtesy of Austin History Center, Austin Public Library C01092

79. Avenue B, west side between 39th Street and 40th Street
pre-1911

Drive through Hyde Park today in search of a body of water and encounter only the small upstream version of Waller Creek. Neighborhood boating enthusiasts will cite Lake Austin, Town Lake, and Lake Travis as nearby locales for pursuing their hobby. Early Hyde Park residents enjoyed an even closer aquatic playground when the man-made Gem Lake was completed in the suburb's southwest corner in 1892. Shortly thereafter the *Austin Daily Statesman* announced additional exciting news in its article describing the upcoming construction of "the long talked of pavilion for Hyde Park." With its spacious maple dance floor, raised seats, and elevated stage, Hyde Park Pavilion would complete the area's transformation into "a grand summer resort."

Avenue B, west side between 39th Street and 40th Street
2004

"Grand" it may have been, but long-lasting the Hyde Park "resort" was not. By 1911 Gem Lake had been filled in and the Pavilion dismantled. That year the school district erected the building in this photograph to replace a smaller frame structure known as Baker School located elsewhere in the neighborhood. The new school building kept the name of the old, which had been in use since 1902 to honor former Austin school inspector DeWitt Baker. In 1940 Baker School upgraded with a new technology now considered a staple of student life, the public address system. Describing the system's advantages in great detail, the *Austin Statesman* noted that every morning "the entire school is joined together in a religious and patriotic observance made possible by the new apparatus . . . thus the day begins at Baker schools [sic] with students paying homage to both God and country, and beginning the work of the day with renewed inspiration." Although the building is no longer used for classes, Baker School continues to serve the Austin school district as a home for the Department of School, Family, and Community Education as well as the Department of School Support Services.

Courtesy of Austin History Center, Austin Public Library C03254

80. 43rd Street at Speedway, northeast corner
1930

Austin firefighters show off their new engine in front of Hyde Park's Fire Station #9. The opening of the firehouse on August 1, 1929, ended decades of worry by area residents. Previously the nearest engine company had been housed well outside the neighborhood in the 3000 block of Guadalupe Street, prompting legitimate fears that firefighters would not be able to reach Hyde Park homes in time to do much good.

43rd Street at Speedway, northeast corner
2004

Citing redundant service and the need for budget restraint, City Council tried twice in the 1970s to close Fire Station #9. Each time local residents fought successfully for preservation of an active engine company in their neighborhood. The annual Fire Station Festival has been held yearly in Hyde Park since 1975 in commemoration of these victories. In 2003 the Hyde Park Neighborhood Association learned of Fire Department plans to replace the full-size engine in the photograph with a "mini-pumper" truck requiring only two crew members instead of the usual four. As noted in the October 2003 Hyde Park Neighborhood Association newsletter *Pecan Press,* "This year our wonderful Austin firefighters gave up their annual raise to save our beloved station. So once again, we will gather at the station to celebrate their victory, and ours."

**81. Avenue B, east side between 44th Street and 45th Street
1920s**

As reported by the *Austin American-Statesman* in January 1983, old-timer Otto Salcher reminisced in the Avenue B Grocery during his first visit to the store in 20 years. "Mr. Harris paid for it (the store) in dimes, buckets of dimes he had saved up. I was renting from him at the time and he used some of my dimes when he bought the store in 1925. He used to sit out under the tree and play dominoes and he would tell you to help yourself. But there wasn't too much to take." Mr. Harris was S.H. Harris, seen in this photograph standing in front of his Hyde Park business. Depending on the source, founder Marshall L. Johnson opened the grocery anywhere between 1903 and 1910.

Avenue B, east side between 44th Street and 45th Street
2004

Avenue B Grocery acquired its name from Bill Stefka's brother-in-law in the 1940s. Stefka bought the business from his relative in 1950, which he and his wife Libbye operated for the next several decades. Such stores were anything but unusual in Hyde Park's early years. According to Libbye Stefka, "When we first got here, there were a jillion stores like this on Speedway." As had other owners, the Stefkas lived in a house connected to the rear of their grocery store. Tenth and current owner Ross Mason sells not only groceries but homemade soup, chili, and sandwiches. His landmark store's continued popularity was evident on a recent visit to the premises at which a breathless Mason was unable to pause even long enough to offer a better time for calling again.

Courtesy of Austin History Center, Austin Public Library C05859

82. Guadalupe Street, east side between 45th Street and 46th Street
1941

"Builders of Beauty and Bringers of Bounty." So boasted a 1927 newspaper advertisement for F. T. Ramsey and Sons Austin Nursery. The man known as "Fruit Tree" Ramsey because of his initials assumed control of the family business after the death of his father Alexander in 1895. The elder Ramsey brought his family to Texas from Mississippi in 1860. He began selling plants and fruit trees in Burnet County in 1875, then moved into a building at Avenue B and 45th Street in Austin in 1894 after being impressed by the prosperity of a fruit orchard he had planted in the area. Business flourished immediately as new homes and customers appeared in the Hyde Park subdivision across the street. At its largest, the nursery covered 430 acres, including what are now the grounds of the State School for the Blind and Visually Impaired and much of Lamar Boulevard. The above photograph appeared on the cover of Ramsey's 1945 catalogue and shows the company's business headquarters at 4525 Guadalupe Street.

Guadalupe Street, east side between 45th Street and 46th Street
2004

Frank Ramsey was a well-known Hyde Park figure for almost 40 years. After his death in 1932, control of the nursery passed to his sons J. M. and Murray Perkins Ramsey. In 1965 Murray halted retail sales and restricted operations to landscape contracting. By that time most of the 430 original acres had been disposed of. Current Austin homeowners must meet their landscaping needs without Ramsey's Nursery. The vacant headquarters building on Guadalupe awaits probable demolition by a new owner. Only a small portion of the long shed in the older photograph remains. Most of the structure was removed to make way for an apartment building hidden behind the trees at left.

H. B. HILLYER, Photographer,

AUSTIN, TEXAS.

Courtesy of Austin History Center, Austin Public Library PICA 04183

83. State Lunatic Asylum
c. 1865

Following a mid-19th century trend in the treatment of mental illness, the Texas Legislature established the State Lunatic Asylum on 380 acres north of Austin in 1856. The main wing (at left in the photograph) opened with twelve patients in 1861. The rest of the structure in this view was completed by 1865. The building's design included insulating stone walls four feet thick, high ceilings, transoms over doors to promote air flow, and rooftop cupolas to entice air currents into the hallways. Construction prompted the Indians living around the lakes at the southern edge of the grounds to move out of the area. A natural spring-fed chain of lakes eventually became the main attraction of a well-manicured park. After Monroe Shipe developed nearby Hyde Park, the Asylum grounds became a popular location for family picnics, carriage rides, rowboat excursions, and other recreational activities.

Austin State Hospital
2004

By 1968 the renamed Austin State Hospital had an average daily population of 3,313 patients. Long a community in its own right, the institution at one time or another had its own schools, clinics, vegetable gardens, kitchens, and facilities for making clothes. A cemetery held the remains of those unclaimed by relatives at death. An off-site dairy and hog farm was established in 1942 to provide milk and meat. But changing treatment of mental illness eventually shrank the hospital census dramatically. The original, renovated asylum building now houses hospital administration. While the grounds still comprise a green island in a sea of residential neighborhoods, the park-like atmosphere diminished with further building construction and draining of the lakes. A substantial portion of the grounds is now leased for commercial use by a shopping mall, apartment complex, and specialty heart hospital.

VI. Out of Town

Before urban sprawl

"Mr. Ramsey would send down a big wagon to the church filled with hay, and everybody piled in for a day in the country . . . there was one favorite place where there were trees, grass, and a running stream . . . after lunch, the boys and men usually went down stream for a swim while the women and girls took off their shoes and stockings, held up their many skirts, and enjoyed a wade in the stream."

— Juliette Wright, early 20th century Austin resident

One hundred years ago an Austin family visiting any of the locations in this chapter would have packed for a day in the country. Reminded by their parents to bring towels and bathing suits, children might also have tossed fishing poles, bait, and tackle next to the picnic basket already in the wagon. At the end of a long, dusty ride the family could find itself spreading a blanket under an oak grove along a clear stream, or struggling up the tallest hill in the area for a magnificent view of the open countryside west of the Colorado River. Parents and children alike would have enjoyed a day of solitude, a day removed from the rush of the city, a day interrupted only occasionally by other travelers.

To reach these sites today many Austin residents would merely spend a few minutes driving their automobiles *toward* the city. Fishing poles and bathing suits would be left at home. Upon arrival there would be no picnicking, fishing, swimming, or wading. Viewing the luxury lakeside homes along the former Colorado River would require ascending about a hundred concrete steps to a covered platform most likely already occupied by several other visitors.

Vast changes have accompanied Austin's growth from a cluster of log huts in a muddy ravine to a sprawling metropolis of asphalt, concrete, and steel. Urban development years ago approached, then surrounded each of the landmarks depicted in the vintage photographs of this chapter. Development obliterated some

landmarks, altered others almost beyond recognition, and left a precious few virtually intact.

Every Austin resident at some point climbs the steps on Mount Bonnell to enjoy the spectacular panoramic view of the city available at its peak. Few, however, understand just how remote this tourist site seemed to their ancestors. In former times Camp Mabry officers led their men on long marches to camp at the hill's base. Even after the automobile's appearance, Mount Bonnell was accessible only by carefully driving up a twisting dirt and gravel road.

State legislators intentionally located the State Lunatic Asylum on land far north of town to provide a more relaxing environment for its inmates. Stores, apartments, and residential neighborhoods now surround the grounds. African-Americans by the thousands once rode in covered wagons to the St. John Encampment for a week-long religious revival in the country. That campground is now a parking lot for one of Austin's first enormous shopping malls. A young Austin couple moved into their family's country cottage on acreage by a Colorado River inlet in 1922. Modern Mayfield Park provides a green oasis in a suburban city neighborhood.

Explore these sites today and remember the pleasing serenity experienced there by Austin's early citizens. Then drive outside of the modern city limits and ponder what that area *should* look like in a later lifetime. The changes we impose often prove to be permanent. What should be preserved and what can be sacrificed? Will our great-grandchildren praise our wisdom or curse our folly? Should we care? *Do* we care?

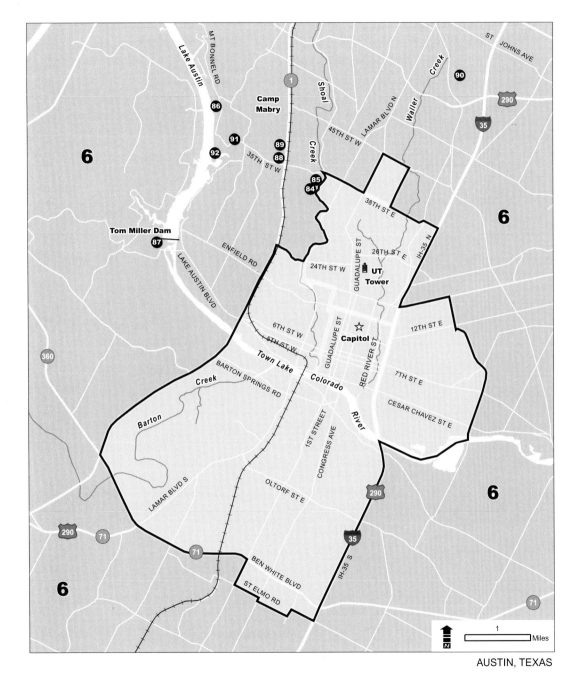

AUSTIN, TEXAS

Courtesy of Austin History Center, Austin Public Library PICA 01904

84. 34th Street, looking west at Shoal Creek
1938

Before invading whites evicted them, local Indians had long followed a well-beaten path along Shoal Creek to this spot near present-day 34th Street. The trail began at a ford near the creek's mouth on the Colorado River and followed the waterway north before crossing over and heading west. Austin area residents constructed a bridge here to span the creek in the 1850s. Wagons then had a route out of town along the public highway leading west. By the time a sturdier concrete bridge was built in 1916, automobiles shared passage with pedestrians, horses, and wagons.

34th Street, looking west at Shoal Creek
2004

In 1939 workers rerouted 34th Street a few feet south during construction of a wider bridge. The 1916 structure remains as a pedestrian walkway across Shoal Creek in the vicinity of the remains of Alamo Dam below Seiders' Springs. Heading south from the bridge, a city hike-and-bike trail follows the old Indian path. What was once Austin's gateway to the west now points toward miles of suburban neighborhoods filled with homes, churches, schools, and shops. Across the creek at right is Shoal Creek Hospital, an in-patient psychiatric facility.

Courtesy of Austin History Center, Austin Public Library C03261

85. Shoal Creek, looking southwest between 34th Street and 38th Street
c. 1890

Pictured here is Seiders' Springs bathhouse, which deteriorated quickly after its closing in 1890. An enterprising Edward Seiders built the resort in 1871 to take advantage of the constant flow of clean, cool water from the cliff-side springs above Shoal Creek. City residents could ride a hack to the site from the Avenue Hotel on Congress Avenue for a day of picnicking and lolling in the pools. A dance platform provided further diversion, while a store and cafe in the two-story building below the springs offered refreshments. Seiders acquired the property through Louisa White, his wife since 1846. Louisa's father Gideon White died in an 1842 fight with local Indians. White had built a cabin beneath an oak grove on the west side of Shoal Creek opposite Seiders Springs. A New York developer bought the property in 1890 with intentions of including it in his planned suburban community of Glen Ridge. He constructed Alamo Dam just north of the State Street (34th Street) bridge to create a small lake complete with swans and rowboats. Glen Ridge never passed beyond the planning stage, while the lake disappeared with Alamo Dam's collapse in a 1900 flood.

Shoal Creek, looking southwest between 34th Street and 38th Street
2004

Although Seiders Springs still trickle out from its banks, Shoal Creek is but a shadow of its former self. Development along most of its course has reduced the waterway to little more than a drainage ditch. Former swimming holes and fishing spots are most often dry or filled with stagnant water. The site of Gideon White's frontier cabin lies in central Austin sandwiched between Seton Medical Center to the east and a supermarket and Shoal Creek Hospital to the west. Although the hike-and-bike trail along the creek remains pretty, one has only to visit Barton Springs, Austin's most famous natural swimming hole, to realize the extent of the city's squandered opportunity.

Courtesy of Austin History Center, Austin Public Library C02335

**86. Mount Bonnell Road, looking north
early 20th century**

Mount Bonnell, the highest natural point in Austin at 780 feet above sea level, has long been a popular destination for the city's inhabitants. At the time of this photograph a bumpy drive up rugged, unpaved Mount Bonnell Road yielded a panoramic view of an almost undeveloped countryside. In the 1830s local residents reportedly referred to the peak as "Antonette's Leap" in memory of a young woman who leapt to her death to escape Indians who had just killed her fiancée. Not long afterward the hill acquired the name of Mount Bonnell. George W. Bonnell came to the state from New York in 1836 to join the fight to wrest Texas from Mexico. He was executed after being captured by the Mexican army as part of the disastrous Mier Expedition into Mexico.

Mount Bonnell Road, looking north
2004

Still a popular tourist destination, Mount Bonnell is currently traversed by a much smoother and busier Mount Bonnell Road. Expensive homes line the lake shore while hills in the background have been overtaken by suburbia. The graceful Loop 360 bridge in the distance helped spur this development by providing a northwestern crossing over Lake Austin. Many of the residents in this area of town are members of the Austin Country Club at the southern end of the bridge (obscured by trees at left).

Courtesy of Austin History Center, Austin Public Library PICA 03847

87. Lake McDonald, viewed from the west end of the Austin Dam
1893-1900

Austin municipal leaders dreamed of transforming their city into a major manufacturing center with the opening of this dam across the Colorado River in 1893. West Texas rancher A. F. Shephard saw a different opportunity. Shephard formed the Lake Navigation Company in July 1891 with the purpose of exploiting "a country that presents scenery of the most romantic and picturesque character." Austin residents watched excitedly as Lake Navigation's twin paddle steamboat *Ben Hur* took shape on the banks of the Colorado River, then waited apprehensively as the new Lake McDonald filled up after the dam's completion. On its maiden voyage in 1893 two thousand passengers thronged the decks of the 181-foot long sternwheeler.

Many danced below in the ship's spacious salon while others lounged comfortably in one of the 30 private cabins on the second deck. At 15 miles per hour the Ben Hur completed two 4-hour round-trips a day. Tickets cost 50 cents apiece. Shephard, however, touted more than the recreational opportunities provided by the *Ben Hur*. Predicting that with Lake McDonald "the fertile valleys along its shores will be transformed into market gardens and orchards," he also envisioned that "farmers living near the lake will be enabled to bring their produce to market in their own wagon and return home the same day . . . this easy method of reaching the city will attract to Austin trade that is now going elsewhere."

Lake Austin, viewed from the west end of Tom Miller Dam
2004

Builders of the Austin Dam did not foresee the huge amount of sediment which the river would deposit against its base. When a 1900 flood augmented the immense pressure created by the sediment, the dam cracked in two places. As the cracks widened under the strain, the entire section in between broke loose and slid downstream. The resulting lake current ripped some boats from their moorings to crash against the dam and immediately capsized others. The *Ben Hur's* size failed to protect it against the raging water. Crew members escaped as the boat broke loose and foundered in 30 feet of water along the west bank of the draining lake. Without the water's support the *Ben Hur* collapsed under her enormous weight, leaving nothing but a twisted skeleton behind for saddened city residents to dwell upon. The city attempted to rebuild the dam in 1915 but ran out of money before completing the project. After yet another devastating flood in 1935 civic leaders tried again, this time with a more satisfying outcome. Tom Miller Dam has successfully held back the waters of Lake Austin for the past 64 years.

Courtesy of Austin History Center, Austin Public Library PICA 16347

88. 35th Street, north side, to the west of the I&GN Railroad tracks
c. 1900

Readers of the July 6, 1892, *Austin Daily Statesman* learned of the establishment of "the finest military encampment grounds in America" on a site west of the city blessed with "high altitude, pure air, and crystal water." Six days later the *Daily Statesman* announced that "a great change has come over the appearance of the old Daxey place . . . trees have been trimmed up, the branches cleared off and all the sticks and stones removed.

The parade ground has been carefully mowed off and is now as fine a stretch of level land as can be found in any portion of the State." Although state Adjutant General W. H. Mabry had the right to name the new camp, he announced a vote in which the soldiers themselves would select the name. Repaying the favor the men chose "Camp Mabry." Austin officially donated the grounds to the state in 1893.

35th Street, north side between Exposition Boulevard and Mopac Expressway
2004

Once-wild Camp Mabry now finds itself surrounded by residential neighborhoods. In front of the camp's main gate, West 35th Street heads west past Mayfield Park toward Mount Bonnell and east over the MoPac Expressway. As they have for over a century, Austinites continue to enjoy parades, re-enactment encampments, and sham battles on the grounds.

Locals also enjoy running on the camp's track and visiting a well-kept military museum. Camp leaders closed the main entrance gate to Camp Mabry (now headquarters of the Texas National Guard) after the attacks in New York City and Washington, D.C. in 2001 (note the concrete barrier). Visitors now enter through a more secure gate farther west on 35th Street.

Courtesy of Austin History Center, Austin Public Library C00741

89. International and Great Northern Railroad tracks, west of the city
post-1915

Talk about explosive politics! Before this building, the State Arsenal, was erected in 1915 the Texas National Guard stored its ammunition three miles away in the basement of the State Capitol. Legislators allocated $20,000 in 1914 for construction, perhaps motivated by the fact that underneath them lay "military stores of every description." The Arsenal was the first permanent structure ever built by the state for the Guard. The International and Great Northern Railroad (I&GN) laid a special switch track from its main line for easy access to the Camp Mabry site.

Mopac Expressway, west side between 38th Street and 45th Street
2004

Known today as Building 41, the old Arsenal currently holds Camp Mabry administrative offices. The rear section of the building and the railroad siding were removed in the 1970s to accommodate the Mopac Expressway. A steady flow of automobile traffic streams by in place of the supply trains which once stopped here. At the request of Camp Mabry security personnel monitoring the area with video cameras, the police officer in the patrol car stopped the photographer for questioning moments after this picture was taken.

Courtesy of Austin History Center, Austin Public Library PICA 04421

90. Four miles north of the city, looking north
post-1907

Tents and horse-drawn wagons mark the site of the St. John Encampment in this photograph. For years thousands of African-Americans journeyed to the annual revival on 303 acres north of Austin owned by the St. John Regular Missionary Baptist Association, a group of central Texas Baptist churches. Donations and loans financed construction of the St. Johns Home for Negro Orphans, later known as the St. Johns Industrial Home for Black Orphans. The stone building pictured here replaced an earlier one destroyed by fire within years of its construction in 1907. The school accommodated 200 children; a separate dormitory housed teachers. Classes ran from first grade through college level. Besides offering entertainment and instruction, the Encampment raised funds for the orphanage. Ella Mae Campbell, whose father-in-law is the namesake of Campbell Elementary School in Austin, recalled, "Everybody who came would bring things like sugar, bed sheets, pillow cases, or beans. Everybody pitched in to help keep the orphanage running."

Clayton Lane, looking north between Airport Boulevard and Middle Fiskville Road
2004

Under a burden of debt accumulated during the Depression, the St. Johns Association closed the orphanage in 1942. Association head the Reverend A. K. Black then began selling housing lots in the area for $50 apiece. The resulting St. John community lay well outside the city, with many residents walking up to two miles to catch the bus at Ridge Top (now East 51st Street) to work in Austin. After World War II the city annexed St. John.

Pressure from surrounding white residents, developers, and city officials finally forced Black to sell the 300 acres around the orphanage in 1956. The building burned that same year. Today Dillard's Department Store in Highland Mall seems to float on an ocean of pavement at the site of the one-time orphanage. The nearby St. John neighborhood remains as a small vestige of its former self.

Courtesy of Austin History Center, Austin Public Library PICH 05834

91. Mayfield-Gutsch House, Old Bull Creek Road
1927

In 1833 Stephen F. Austin wrote to his friend Samuel May Williams of his intention to retire to "land on the east side of the Colorado at the foot of the mountains," ambition destroyed by Austin's early death in 1836. Polly Carlton and her husband Fred inherited ninety-five acres of this tract in 1874. The Carletons may have constructed the country cottage in this photograph in the early 1890s in anticipation that upcoming dam construction would create a lakefront location. Or Texas Railroad Commission chairman Allison Mayfield may have built the house during an Austin construction boom after his purchase of the property in 1909 for $1,305. Of Mayfield, Congressman and future Vice President John Nance Garner once said, "He is too modest, and that is the only fault I can find with him." After moving into the home in 1920, Mayfield lived only another three years. He bequeathed the house and its 28 $^3/_4$ acres to his only child, daughter Mary Mayfield Gutsch. Mary and husband Milton, a long-time University of Texas history professor and department chairman, had lived in the country cottage since 1922.

212

Mayfield-Gutsch House, Old Bull Creek Road
2004

A 1927 gossip columnist noted that "out at the Allison Mayfield place pretty Mary Gutsch watches her garden grow." With help over the years from Milton and resident gardener Steve Arredondo, Mary expanded existing gardens, added many others, constructed stone walls and lily ponds, and planted thousands of flowers and exotic plants. The Gutsches received two Blue India Peacocks for Christmas one year; by 1950 the grounds held 35 peacocks of four different varieties. When Milton died in 1967 a university press release noted that "class attendance (for his lectures) was near-perfect, especially just before the Christmas vacation, when Professor Gutsch always sang student drinking songs from the Middle Ages." Mary lived another four years after her husband's death, spending much of that time as she always had, working on her beloved gardens. In a hand-written will she decreed, "the home and acreage is left to the City of Austin as a park to be used for no other purpose-not to be used by any other organization-otherwise it shall be given to the Austin Travis County Humane Society." Mrs. Gutsch also stated that the property be designated Mayfield Park. An extensive effort in 1988 by Gregg Free restored Mayfield Park, along with its shaded walks, lily ponds, and exotic peacocks, to its former status as a secluded country retreat.

Courtesy of Austin History Center, Austin Public Library C10767 Pano

92. Laguna Gloria, east shore of Lake Austin
c. 1920

An unidentified group of elegant women gathers at the home of Clara and Hal Sevier. The couple bought 28.5 acres on the Colorado River in 1915 for $4,750 and completed this Mediterranean villa on the property the following year. The land originally was part of the much larger tract purchased in 1835 by Stephen F. Austin. Austin died before utilizing the site, which lay vacant throughout the rest of the 19th century. Clara and Hal called their winter home Laguna Gloria after a beautiful nearby lagoon formed by the river, as well as La Gloria, a large ranch owned by Clara's cattleman father Robert Driscoll. One-time Texas state legislator Hal Sevier had founded and was editor of the *Austin American* at the time of Laguna Gloria's construction. Clara Driscoll Sevier had gained fame in 1903 through her purchase of the Alamo in San Antonio, thereby saving the cherished landmark from demolition.

Austin Museum of Art at Laguna Gloria, east shore of Lake Austin
2004

After the death of Clara's brother in 1929 she moved with her husband to Corpus Christi to manage the Driscoll family's business interests. The Seviers entrusted their Austin house to the care of a Mexican caretaker named Galvan. Franklin Roosevelt appointed Sevier Ambassador to Chile in 1933. Upon returning to the United States in 1937 Hal and Clara divorced, with Clara reclaiming her maiden name of Driscoll. Obstruction of the Colorado River in 1940 with Tom Miller Dam inundated 10 acres of Laguna Gloria's grounds. Three years later Clara Driscoll donated the house and remaining 18.5 acres to the Texas Fine Arts Holding Corporation with the stipulation that the property be maintained as an art museum. In partnership with other local art museums, Laguna Gloria formed the Austin Museum of Art in 1992 and changed its name to the Austin Museum of Art at Laguna Gloria.

VII. Around the 40 Acres

"A university of the first class"

"The Legislature shall, as soon as practicable, establish, organize, and provide for the maintenance, support, and direction of a university of the first class, to be located by a vote of the people of this State, and styled 'The University of Texas' . . . ."

— Article VII, Texas Constitution of 1876

"Smite the rocks with the rod of knowledge, and fountains of unstinted wealth will gush forth."

— Ashbel Smith, president of the University of Texas board of regents, at the school's opening ceremony in 1881

Dr. Ashbel Smith must have had a true passion for education. How else to explain his exuberant claim to the crowd attending his November 1882 address atop College Hill in north Austin? "The cornerstone of The University of Texas now about to be laid far surpasses in solemn importance and in weighty, widely diffusive and long reaching consequences, any cornerstone of any building hitherto laid, or likely hereafter to be laid, in the broad territory among the future millions of Texas."

Texas legislators had directed that land be set aside for a university in the republic's new capital way back in 1839. Nineteen years later the state finally made an effort to fund the school, but the Civil War disrupted those plans. A new state constitution in 1876 again specified that a state university be established, this time in a city selected by Texas voters. Alexander Wooldridge and Jacob Fontaine were two of many prominent Austin residents leading the campaign to put the university in the state capital. Wooldridge became secretary of the school's first board of regents. African-American Fontaine had a right to feel used. Although the Legislature had mandated a state college or branch university for blacks, it specifically forbade a new tax or diversion of funds from the main school to pay for it.

Dr. Smith made his bold claim in 1882 while standing in an empty field. The earliest photographs of the university show little more than a few scattered buildings breaking the monotony of the landscape. Worn dirt footpaths connect the structures. A postcard from the era shows several young women relaxing in a broad sea of bluebonnets with the Old Main Building in the background.

George Brackenridge donated 445 acres along the Colorado River in southwest Austin to the University of Texas in 1910. When the Board of Regents decided that the university's original 40 acres no longer sufficed it voted to move the campus to the donated land. After a contentious battle pitting the Chamber of Commerce and local newspaper editors against campus-area businesses and residents, the school decided to stay put.

But the 40 acres still weren't enough. In the decades that followed, the university gobbled up large chunks of land, primarily to the east and south. Entire residential neighborhoods disappeared to accommodate the expanding campus. University land now reaches as far south as East 15th Street and as far north as East 30th Street. The campus extends across Interstate Highway 35 to Comal Street in East Austin. Only the western boundary has remained constant at Guadalupe Street, known by locals as "the Drag."

Those off-campus areas with closest ties to university life lie west and north of the school. Textbook stores and other businesses geared toward student needs line Guadalupe Street. The neighborhood beyond

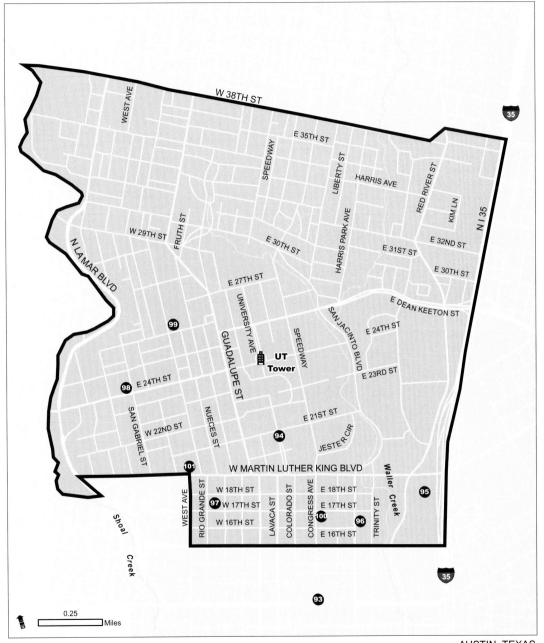

is filled with fraternity and sorority houses, apartments, and a few scattered high-rise student residences. A recently announced city plan calls for major changes, however, with higher density apartment towers replacing many of the smaller buildings.

The area north of campus has perhaps changed the least over the years. Modest homes provide housing for many university faculty and staff. Southward expansion has run up against the northward extension of the Capitol complex and surrounding government buildings. Houses, churches, and small businesses were squeezed out many years ago. Stadiums for the men's baseball and women's softball teams lie across the freeway in East Austin. The University of Texas Press also operates on the other side of Interstate Highway 35. Historic and modern ties of surrounding neighborhoods to the rest of East Austin are stronger than those with the university.

This chapter covers a large and extremely varied region of Austin. A first glance at the sites in these photographs suggests only a random collection of buildings and streets. The University of Texas, however, is and has long been a city itself within the City of Austin. Its impact on the urban landscape extends well beyond the boundaries of its own real estate. Around the 40 acres then, one cannot help but encounter history as shaped by the state's "university of the first class."

AUSTIN, TEXAS

Courtesy of Austin History Center, Austin Public Library PICA 19239

93. North view from the dome of the Capitol Building
c. 1890

When the Republic of Texas established a capital on the Colorado River in 1839 it directed that land in the area be set aside for a state institution of higher learning. This view from the Capitol dome looks out over the selected site, a 40-acre hilltop situated north of the original city boundary. Shortly after Texas voters chose Austin over several other cities as the home of the university in 1881, construction began on Old Main, first building of the University of Texas. In this photograph a partially completed Old Main (1)

marks the center of an otherwise empty campus. Note two other significant structures. Turn Verein Hall (Turner Hall), built by a German social club in 1871, is the asymmetric, elongated building with the left-sided peaked roof seen just above the center left portion of the photograph (2). A city directory advertisement appearing in 1872 boasted of it as "the finest hall and stage in the state." The Swedish Lutheran Church (3) occupies the southwest corner of Congress Avenue (leading away from the Capitol at right) and 16th Street.

North view from the dome of the Capitol Building
2004

A new Old Main, more commonly referred to as the UT Tower, replaced the first Old Main in the 1930s. Having expanded from the original 40 acres to 350 acres, the university campus now has its own skyline to rival that of the surrounding city. Turner Hall has become a Scottish Rite Temple. It is almost completely obstructed in the photograph by a parking garage. The building was purchased by Ben Hur Shrine Temple in 1912 and transferred to Scottish Rite of Freemasonry in 1914. Having survived the demolition of its surrounding residential neighborhood, the Swedish Lutheran Church today is home to the Texas Historical Commission. In the left foreground is the Texas Supreme Court Building, which was constructed in 1954 with revenue left over from the Texas Confederate Pension Fund.

Courtesy of Austin History Center, Austin Public Library PICA C06260

94. University Avenue, looking north at West 21st Street
1911

"It was a proud day indeed, when the announcement was made that the University was ready for us. It was not quite complete, but it seemed wonderful indeed to us, and we felt that every other student in the country would envy us in the possession of such a magnificent building." When University of Texas student Will L. Vining spoke of this "magnificent building" in 1884, he was of course referring to Old Main, the first structure erected for the new state university. Designed by Millett Opera House architect Frederik Ruffini, Old Main proved to be the last great project of Master Builder Abner Cook. Among Cook's many other successes were the Governor's Mansion, the Sampson-Henricks Building, and Woodlawn, Elisha Pease's plantation home. Cook actually built only Old Main's west wing. He died before the central section (1891) and east wing (1899) were added. Old Main stood atop College Hill, which had previously been covered with live oak and mesquite trees. Initially the school's *only* building, Old Main provided classrooms, lecture halls, and a grand auditorium for the university's first students.

University Avenue, looking north at West 21st Street
2004

"That steam shovel shrieking and grunting is digging your grave—proudly descend." This is the last line of English professor M. N. Posey's poetic tribute to "The Parthenon of the University's Acropolis," otherwise known as Old Main. Although many protested the 1930s demolition of UT's first and most-beloved building, the Board of Regents ultimately decided that restoration would prove too costly. The "New Main" building, now more commonly called "the UT tower," opened in 1937 as the university's library. An early effort to reassemble Old Main's tower elsewhere eventually fizzled. University gardeners preserved the historic building's ivy in the campus greenhouse; many of today's campus ivy-covered walls display the results. Old Main's bricks survive in numerous houses throughout Austin. Some of the bricks even found their way into New Main when they were used to line the building's wind shafts. The UT Tower survived a fire in its upper floors in 1965. A year later Charles Whitman darkened local history when he killed 16 people and wounded 30 with a sniper's rifle from atop the tower. After yet another suicide leap in 1975, the university closed the observation deck to visitors. When UT constructed an enclosure to prevent further suicides and reopened the deck to sightseers in 1998, it restored one of Austin's most impressive visual experiences. The UT Tower is today a beloved city landmark, as inextricably linked to the school's identity as was its Gothic predecessor.

Courtesy of Austin History Center, Austin Public Library PICA 18303

95. Between Red River Street and East Avenue, looking north from south of 19th Street
post-1867

In 1856 the Texas Legislature established a state Blind Asylum and solicited bids for a facility north of Austin. Charles F. Millett collected the $100 prize for submitting the best plan. Master Builder Abner Cook's bid of $8,045 was accepted for construction of the original building, much altered by the time of this photograph. After the Civil War, General George Custer and family resided briefly in the asylum, praised by Mrs. Custer for having "room enough for all the staff, and a long saloon parlor and dining room for our hops [dances] during the winter." The renamed Blind Institute resumed operations on the premises in 1867 with five students. Enrollment had grown to 230 by the time of the school's move to a new campus on 45th Street in 1915.

Between Red River Street and Interstate Highway 35, looking north from south of Martin Luther King Jr. Boulevard
2004

The University of Texas leased the old Blind Institute for use as a School of Military Aeronautics during World War I. In 1926 the former asylum, along with several more recently-built surrounding structures, was transferred permanently to the university. Known as Little Campus Dormitory, the complex housed college students for the next 36 years. The end of the building's life seemed near in 1970 according to an article in *Waterloo Scrapbook*, which noted matter-of-factly that the entire complex "is doomed to come down before long." UT preserved the historic Blind Institute during a major renovation in 1984 (and restored it to its original appearance), but demolished the buildings around it. Now named for former university dean Arno Nowotny, the restored Blind Asylum appears today as it did in Custer's time.

Courtesy of Austin History Center, Austin Public Library PICA 08823

96. San Jacinto Boulevard, east side between 16th Street and 17th Street
pre-1885

Only 15 years after opening his Germania Beer Garden in 1866, German-born August Scholz was already billing his establishment as "The Oldest Beer Garden in the State." City residents were invited to "The place where you can go, at all times, and enjoy a quiet retreat with your friends." Nineteenth-century Austin was home to several popular beer gardens besides Scholz's. According to one long-time citizen reminiscing in the 1930s, these gathering spots were "places where you went to drink pleasantly, not to get drunk. You took the family along. And the food they had! You don't know what good food is these days!" The extended Scholz family lived in houses surrounding the beer garden and worked all week preparing dishes for Sunday patrons. These weekend extravaganzas offered not only good food and drink, but music, plays, bowling, fireworks, military drills, and other amusements. As Scholz prospered, he involved himself in civic affairs. He was a city councilman 1873-1875, a local election officer in 1878, and an official University of Texas fund-raiser in 1883. In 1893 the Longhorn football team celebrated its first undefeated season with a party at Scholz's Garden.

San Jacinto Boulevard, east side between 16th Street and 17th Street
2004

In 1885 August Scholz turned over management of the Garden to his son-in-law, bandleader Carl William Besserer. He and wife Mary inherited the property when Scholz died six years later. By 1893 Besserer wished to devote more of his time to music and sold the Garden to Lemp Brewery of Saint Louis, makers of Falstaff beer. Besserer's band continued to provide Sunday afternoon entertainment. The Austin Saengerrunde, a German singing society, began a relationship with Scholz's in 1892 that continues to this day when it began holding occasional practices in the bowling alley. Nine years later the Saengerrunde moved permanently onto the premises. Society membership proved popular in part because it provided an opportunity to obtain beer on Sunday at a time when state "blue laws" kept the bars closed. The Saengerrunde purchased Scholz's from Lemp in 1908. In the 20th century Scholz's became a popular watering hole for state politicians. When UT attempted to acquire the building for a student union in 1963, owner Bob Bales persuaded the Legislature to pass a law killing the idea. Scholz Garten today boasts not of being the oldest beer garden in the state, but "the oldest continually operating business in Texas"!

Courtesy of Austin History Center, Austin Public Library C09234

**97. West 17th Street, north side between Nueces Street and Rio Grande Street
1936**

In the late 19th century sugar planter Littleberry A. Ellis built the four-story twenty-room Victorian mansion partially hidden behind the trees at left. Between 1910 and 1916 the house held a girls' school but became a private home again in 1918 for junior high school principal Joseph Simmons. Two years later the private Physicians and Surgeons Hospital took over the building. After forming a corporation to manage the hospital in 1924, a group from St. David's Episcopal Church renamed the hospital for their house of worship. When St. David's Hospital added the 46-bed facility in the center of the photograph in 1928 it turned the old mansion into a home for nurses. In her newspaper column *Waterloo Scrapbook*, Audray Bateman described the "home-like atmosphere" of the hospital in those days. "On a cold winter day there were always cheery fires burning in the huge fireplaces, and the rooms were more like bedrooms in a home than sterile hospital rooms."

West 17th Street, north side between Nueces Street and Rio Grande Street
2004

Architect Louis F. Southerland described the Victorian mansion he demolished to make way for Rio House Apartments in 1961 by recalling, "It was four stories, had about 20 rooms, and was beautifully constructed. . . I hated to see it come down but there just wasn't any use for it. . . ." Southerland's firm of Page, Southerland, and Page saw more utility in razing the old home, gutting the 1928 hospital building and covering the structure's facade with a wire screen, and incorporating what remained into its new apartment complex. The Texas Society of Architects must have agreed, for it bestowed a merit award upon Page, Southerland, and Page for "one of the best designs by Texas architects completed during the past five years." All of this became possible when St. David's Hospital sold its original site in favor of a much larger facility on East 32nd Street in 1954.

Courtesy of Austin History Center, Austin Public Library PICH 05424

98. West 24th Street at San Gabriel Street, northwest corner
20th century

"The gold dollar is the name of this little Paper. Its name taken from A gold dollar which was presented to me by my sister nelly miller on a viset to Mississippi in 1872 as we had been sepperrated by the evel of Slavery for twenty years. this gold dollr I have traded with sence that time and made sixty dollars of it with which I have bought this little Office and started this little Paper." So wrote the Reverend Jacob "Jake" Fontaine, former slave and Baptist preacher, in the inaugural edition of *The Gold Dollar* in August 1876. Fontaine published the first black-owned newspaper in Austin from his home at the corner of San Gabriel Street and Orange (now West 24th) Street. He arrived in Austin in 1839 as the property of President Lamar's personal secretary, the Reverend Edward Fontaine. By the early 1860s Jacob Fontaine was preaching to African-Americans in the basement of the Methodist church at Brazos Street and East Tenth Street. At the same time he also met in secret with members of his own First Baptist Church to plan a split from the white congregation. In 1867 Fontaine helped organize the St. John Regular Missionary Baptist Association. Over the next two decades he founded five additional churches in the area. One of these, New Hope Baptist Church, first met in Fontaine's home. The Reverend was also an early advocate for placing the University of Texas in Austin. He traveled extensively throughout the state to rally black support for this cause.

West 24th Street at San Gabriel Street, northwest corner
2004

Freedman George Franklin built Jacob Fontaine's future home in 1869. Down the street lived James Wheat, founder of the black community of Wheatville in which the Reverend Fontaine lived until his death in 1898. At the beginning of the 20th century Wheatville peaked at about 300 inhabitants. As Austin expanded toward and then surrounded the community, many Italian immigrants moved into the neighborhood. Salvatore Perrone bought what is now called the Franzetti Building in 1905 to house a grocery store. After gaining ownership in 1919, Joe Franzetti operated his own grocery on the premises for almost 50 years. By then Wheatville was no longer an identifiably separate community, in part due to an effective city policy aimed at concentrating blacks in East Austin. Although Ersilia Franzetti and her two children still lived in the former grocery at the time, a 1974 *Austin American-Statesman* article stated that local residents wondered why "the ancient stone building at 2402 San Gabriel, evidently deserted, has not been restored or torn down." Shortly after historic designation by the city in 1977, the structure barely survived being destroyed by a fire. Still owned by Joe Franzetti's descendants, the Franzetti Building today is home to an imported furnishings store.

Courtesy of Austin History Center, Austin Public Library C07895

**99. West 26th Street, north side between Rio Grande Street and Nueces Street
1922**

Distressed by "discourtesies regarding religious matters" facing Catholics undergoing treatment at City-County Hospital, the St. Vincent's Aid Society in 1897 asked the Daughters of Charity of St. Vincent de Paul to operate a new hospital in Austin. When the Daughters agreed, the Society raised $5,300 for purchase of approximately 5 acres of land on 26th Street between Nueces Street and Rio Grande Street. Granted a state charter on April 4, 1900, Seton Infirmary opened two years later with 17 private rooms, 11 wards, and separate dormitories for the Sisters. The infirmary's name honored Elizabeth Ann Seton, founder of the Daughters of Charity. A contemporary publicity pamphlet offered treatment for "all well-intentioned persons."

West 26th Street, north side between Rio Grande Street and Nueces Street
2004

Needing more space, Seton Hospital built a new facility on West 38th Street in 1975. The elegant, original Seton Infirmary building was demolished soon afterward to make way for the mundane apartment complex in this photograph. Younger renters may wonder about the origin of the name of the street which approaches their building from the south, Seton Avenue. Seton Healthcare Network today operates six area hospitals, as well a number of clinics and specialty centers.

Courtesy of Austin History Center, Austin Public Library C01623

100. Congress Avenue, looking south at 16th Street
1892

At one time the area north of the Capitol Building was residential. The horse and diagonal footpath in the empty square bounded by 16th Street, 17th Street, Congress Avenue, and Brazos Street even give the landscape a rural appearance. Behind the trees at left between 14th Street and the Capitol Building is St. Martin's German Lutheran Church. The smokestack of the Capitol power plant sticks up at extreme left.

Congress Avenue, looking south at 16th Street
2004

Over the years state government encroachment from the south and University of Texas growth from the north squeezed the residential neighborhood out of existence. Capitol grounds expansion to 15th street resulted in the demolition of many houses and several churches. State office buildings such as the Robert Johnson Building (at left in this photograph) now take up much of the space between the Capitol complex and the University of Texas. Government employees park their cars where in former times children played and horses grazed. The Frost Bank Tower (between the Capitol dome and the Robert Johnson Building) provides a hint of the modern downtown business district on the far side of the Capitol.

Courtesy of Austin History Center, Austin Public Library C01524

101. West 19th Street at Rio Grande Street, northwest corner
1927

F. Scott Fitzgerald could have been referring to the Wooten family of early Austin when he wrote, "The rich are not like you and I." For not many Austinites then or now could match Thomas Wooten's 1898 wedding gift of the mansion in this photograph to his son Goodall and new daughter-in-law Ella. Thomas Wooten was a prominent surgeon in town who served on the first Board of Regents of the University of Texas. He relocated to Austin from Paris (Texas, not France) in 1872 with his family, which included 3-year-old Goodall. Like his father, UT graduate Goodall studied medicine; he graduated from the New York College of Physicians and Surgeons in 1895. After moving into the $8,100 house, Dr. and Mrs. Wooten spent $10,000 in 1910 adding south and east galleries, extending the west end of the building, and adding a second-floor bedroom and bathroom for daughter Lucie. Under Mrs. Wooten's direction, Nieman-Marcus carried out a $10,000 interior decoration in 1925 in which the house received Austin's first wall-to-wall carpeting. An avid gardener, Mrs. Wooten also had the block surrounding the house extensively landscaped. The first azaleas planted in the city graced the lawns of the Wooten mansion.

Martin Luther King Jr. Boulevard at Rio Grande Street, northwest corner
2004

Two years after the death of her husband in 1942, Ella Wooten sold her mansion to Fred Adams of Adams Extract fame and moved into the Driskill Hotel. She died in 1972 at age 94. Adams converted the property into a sorority house to help ease the wartime housing crunch around the university. After several ownership changes the house was purchased by DeLois Faulkner in 1979, who remodeled it for use as a drug and alcohol rehabilitation center beginning in 1983. Faulkner's for-profit center ultimately proved unsuccessful despite the plush accommodations. In 2003 Bill Gurasich reopened the mansion as a hotel and restaurant, The Mansion at Judge's Hill. The Wooten home today stands as testimony to the value of historic preservation. Years ago, one far-sighted seller of the property noted, "An obvious 'highest and best use' of the site would probably be to destroy the old buildings and build a residential facility or office building. We feel, however, that this alternative is short-sighted and unnecessarily harsh . . . . As Austin grows and becomes a tourist and convention center, as well as the home of a growing State complex, the buyer will have property as valuable and irreplaceable as the Driskill, Carrington Home, Symphony Square, Heritage House and others."

AFTERWORD

In the early stages of planning this book I found myself driving through East Austin to acquaint myself with a part of our city relatively unknown to me at the time. Approaching downtown along East 6th Street, I parked my car in front of one of the few local establishments I was familiar with, El Milagro Tortilla Factory. The wonderful aroma of Mexican spices and freshly-made corn tortillas greeted me as I entered. As is my habit, I slowly perused the shelves of foreign canned and baked goods before selecting a chilled glass bottle of soda from the cooler. While waiting to pay I listened attentively to the conversation in Spanish between the clerk and the customer ahead of me, making use of my own limited Spanish in a partially successful attempt to understand. Outside, I stood on the sidewalk, sipping my drink and looking around appreciatively at the community so superficially different from my own suburban neighborhood.

Then I saw it. An old, faded, intriguing structure across the street. Surrounded by a makeshift chain-link fence, the building was obviously abandoned. Only a large for-sale sign gave proof that the site was not entirely forgotten. Despite peeling paint and a rubble-strewn driveway the building appeared solid and dignified. A curved, graceful facade helped disguise the structure's simplicity and utilitarian design. Ignorant of the empty building's past, I at least knew that a previous owner had cared about its appearance.

Shortly thereafter I was pleasantly surprised to find a photograph of my discovery at the Austin History Center (see page 134). The 70-year-old view frames a line of taxis in front of Moreno Service Station occupying the eastern portion of the building. Garage owner Nash Moreno is one of several men in the photograph. Adjacent to the service station is the Casino Bar, while a grocery store fills the rest of the structure. This was the Buratti-Moreno Building, Buratti being David Buratti, founder of the grocery which served East Austin from 1905 to 1963.

Over the following weeks I kept a watchful eye on "my" building. I had learned of the owner's desire to destroy the landmark in favor of a high-tech facility and despaired of one day driving by to see an empty lot. I met others who shared my concern. While shooting photographs of the site one day, I was approached by a man who worked in the office I stood in front of. He introduced me to several colleagues, all of whom expressed hope that the Buratti-Moreno building would be restored.

Subsequently I met with Gregg Free to introduce him to my project. Flipping through my collection of photographs, he paused at the one featuring the Buratti-Moreno Building and commented, "It's a shame that building was demolished." In disbelief I later drove to the site and confirmed the depressing truth. A century-old landmark was indeed gone, swept away for lack of will and imagination.

The Buratti-Moreno Building was not architecturally significant. There was no grandeur in its design or execution. No one rich, powerful, or famous called it home. And yet I submit that this structure was as important to our city's history as the finest Abner Cook edifice. Buratti's grocery store was an integral part of the fabric of East Austin life for almost six decades, as well as one of the few physical remainders of early Italian immigration to Austin. Nash Moreno was a respected Mexican-American businessman, whose hard work and generosity enhanced not only his neighborhood, but the entire city. Roy's Taxi, which spent its early years sharing space in Moreno's garage, found success by ignoring racial taboos and offering service to all comers. The business thrives today under the care of Roy Velasquez' children.

Why would a building without magnificence, without design significance, and without connection to someone rich, powerful, or famous be important? I propose this is because history is made by all of us. True, Austin would not exist without well-known Texans such as Mirabeau Lamar and Edwin Waller. But Austin would also not exist without the 200 anonymous laborers who built the first log structures along Congress Avenue. Austin would not exist without the enslaved African-Americans who built many of the early streets and houses in the city. And Austin would not exist without the thousands of people like David Buratti, Nash Moreno, and Roy Velasquez who provided needed services, neighborhood stability, and local economic opportunities. In short, history is made by community, and the Buratti-Moreno Building was, until its destruction, an essential link to the East Austin community of the past. Only if our past bears no relation to our present, and thus no relevance to our future, is the loss of this landmark without meaning.

ACKNOWLEDGMENTS

This book has been my enjoyable hobby for the past 15 months. I would like to thank the following people and institutions for indulging and assisting me.

My wife Sharon, for her constant support and patience.

My children David and Laura, for understanding the need of their father to hog the family computer.

My brother Doug Kerr, for his excellent suggestions regarding the introduction.

My sister Jackie Peace and mother Jeannette Kerr, for believing I could do this.

My literary agent Kathleen Davis Niendorff, for giving me the confidence to achieve success in the face of self-doubt and uncertainty.

Gregg Free, who generously donated his valuable time in writing the foreword.

Ricardo Puente, for the excellent maps of Austin he created for the book.

The staff members of the Austin History Center, for their unfailing helpfulness and expertise. Special thanks to photo curator Margaret Schlankey.

The Austin History Center, for permission to use so many of its historic photographs.

The Center for American History at the University of Texas, for permission to use several historic photographs from its collection.

Chris Currens of the State Preservation Board, for a most interesting trip to the top of the Capitol dome; Ali Turley of the State Preservation Board, for her assistance in obtaining permission for the Capitol dome trip; and the State Preservation Board, for granting access to the top of the Capitol dome.

Jane Burazer of the Austin Water and Wastewater Utility, for her assistance with the Tom Miller Dam photograph.

Sherry Dalton and the Texas Osteopathic Medical Association, for being most helpful in my research of the Bartholomew-Robinson Building.

Tim Finley, for allowing me access to his office at the top of the Scarbrough Building.

The many friends and acquaintences who offered such kind words of encouragement.

SELECTED BIBLIOGRAPHY

Art Work of Austin. Chicago, 1894.

Austin Board of Trade. *The Industrial Advantages of Austin, Texas.* Austin, Akehurst Publishing Company, 1894.

Bateman, Audray. *Waterloo Scrapbook.* Austin, Friends of the Austin Public Library, 1976.

Brown, Frank. *Annals of Travis County and the City of Austin.* Austin, 1892-1913.

Erickson, Virginia, and McBee, Sue Brandt. *Austin: The Past Still Present.* Austin, Austin Heritage Society, 1975.

Gray, Judge George H. *Outline History of Austin.* Austin City Directory, Austin, 1872.

Hafertepe, Kenneth. *Abner Cook Master Builder on the Texas Frontier.* Austin, Texas Historical Association, 1992.

Hart, Katherine. *Waterloo Scrapbook.* Austin, Friends of the Austin Public Library, 1968-1975.

Humphrey, David C. and Crawford, Jr., William C. *Austin An Illustrated History.* Sun Valley, California, American Historical Press, 2001.

Jackson, A.T. *Mills of Yesteryear.* El Paso, Texas Western Press, 1971.

Journal of Texas Shortline Railroads and Transportation. Aug., Sept., Oct. 1998 Volume 3 Number 2.

Koch, Augustus. *Bird's-eye View of Austin.* 1887.

Koch, Augustus. *Bird's-eye View of the City of Austin Travis County, Texas.* 1873.

Sitton, Sarah and Sitton, Thad. *Austin's Hyde Park. . . the first 50 years: 1891-1941.* Austin, Pecan Press Publications, 1991.

Texas State Historical Association. *The Handbook of Texas Online.* http://www.tsha.utexas.edu/handbook/online/

Williamson, Roxanne Kuter. *Austin, Texas An American Architectural History.* San Antonio, Trinity University Press, 1973.

INDEX

ORDER FORM

Number of hardbound books @ $39.95 each   _____

Number of soft cover books @ $24.95 each   _____

Less 5% discount with 10 or more   _____

Subtotal   _____

Tax = 8.25% (Texas residents only)   _____

Shipping and handling ($3.95 for first book,
add $1.50 for each additional copy)   _____

(For bulk purchases email
for shipping discount)   _____

TOTAL ORDER   _____

Send check to:
Promised Land Books
6805 Edgefield Drive
Austin, Texas 78731
email: jkerr8@austin.rr.com
www.austinthenandnow.com

Ship to: _____
(Name)

_____
(Street address)

_____
(City, State, Zip)